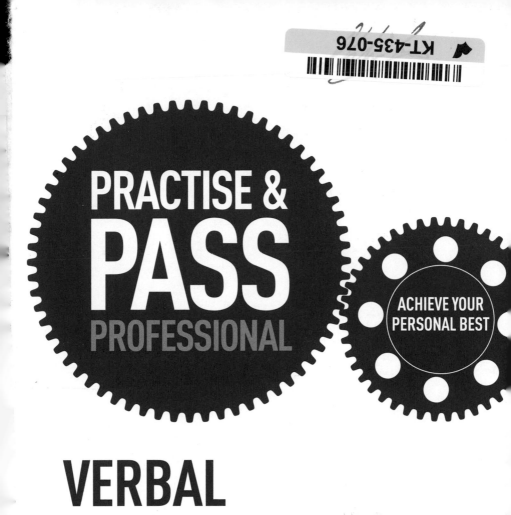

PRACTISE & PASS
PASS
PROFESSIONAL

ACHIEVE YOUR PERSONAL BEST

VERBAL REASONING TESTS

ALAN REDMAN

Acknowledgements

The practice questions in this book are based on real psychometric tests of verbal ability developed by Criterion Partnership, a leading UK-based test publisher, and used by a wide range of employers. I would like to thank Criterion Partnership for making these materials available to readers of this book.

Practise & Pass Professional: Verbal Reasoning Tests

This edition first published in 2010 by Trotman Publishing, a division of Crimson Publishing Ltd., Westminster House, Kew Road, Richmond, Surrey TW9 2ND

© Trotman, 2010

Author Alan Redman

British Library Cataloguing in Publication Data
A catalogue record for this book is available from the British Library

ISBN 978 1 84455 245 0

Printed and bound in the UK by Ashford Colour Press, Gosport, Hants

CONTENTS

INTRODUCTION

WHAT'S IN THIS BOOK?

Working through all the chapters in this book will help you practise and pass verbal tests and answer any questions or anxieties you have about being tested. Here's what lies in store within each chapter.

Chapter 1 Why do you have to take a test anyway?

This chapter sets the scene by providing some background insights into why verbal tests are used and how employers might use the results, before describing how to get the most from working through the remaining chapters of this book.

Chapter 2 Developing your personal best score

Here we explore the concept of your personal best score and how you can maximise your performance on verbal tests. This chapter describes the range of possible strategies for practising and passing verbal tests and provides detailed insider information about the mechanics of verbal testing and how to make testing work to your benefit. This chapter is the key to success as it explains the winning approach you should take to achieve success.

Chapter 3 Verbal comprehension practice questions

Don't be tempted to turn to this chapter straightaway – you'll only achieve maximum benefit from the practice questions in this book if you work through chapters 1 and 2 first. This chapter contains some easier verbal practice questions, which are a valuable place to begin your practice once you have understood how to develop a successful approach in the earlier chapters.

Chapter 4 Verbal reasoning practice questions

We turn up the temperature in this chapter as we introduce more advanced practice questions that measure your verbal reasoning. These questions are best attempted once you have already completed the earlier chapters and the questions in Chapter 3. Along with the right answers, this chapter also provides clear explanations about the reasoning required to arrive at the correct result.

Chapter 5 Verbal critical-reasoning practice questions

These practice questions are representative of the most challenging level of testing used by employers. This chapter contains a series of short tests of your verbal critical reasoning, which even if you're not expecting to face them in real life will help you realise your personal best score through the practice and advice provided.

Chapter 6 Online verbal testing

It is increasingly likely that if you are asked to complete a verbal test you will need to do it online. This chapter provides specific advice about internet-based tests and how you need to adapt the approach and strategies that you would use for paper and pencil testing. This chapter provides detailed insider information about how the online tests work, how they are used and why cheats never prosper!

Chapter 7 What happens after taking the test?

Even when the test is over it's not time to relax! This chapter explains the way in which test scores are calculated and how the results will be fed back to you. We also explore ways in which you can use your verbal test results to improve your future performance when tested again.

Chapter 8 Your testing rights

As a test taker you should expect to be treated in an appropriate manner by the test user. This chapter describes what your rights are when being tested and what you should expect to happen from beginning to end of the testing process. This chapter also contains frequently asked test-taker questions to help put your worries to rest.

Chapter 9 Further resources

There is more help out there that you can access to build on the development you achieve through working through this book. This final chapter provides details of test publishers and professional testing bodies who can offer further advice and help.

GETTING THE MOST FROM THIS BOOK

This book will help you enjoy the potential benefits of taking a verbal test by enabling you to practise and pass. To get the most from the book you should resist the temptation to jump directly to the practice questions. Chapter 2 has important advice for developing your test performance and will help guide your approach to improving your score.

Chapters 3, 4 and 5 contain practice questions for the three different levels of difficulty that verbal ability tests measure. You should work through these in order regardless of the type of verbal test you will take in future – completing all three chapters of practice questions will help you to maximise your test performance.

CHAPTER 1
WHY DO YOU HAVE TO TAKE A TEST ANYWAY?

Nobody likes taking tests, with the possible exception of a few over-achievers and masochists, but they are an increasing fact of life. Schoolchildren are now tested from an early age, our life choices are significantly influenced through the academic assessments we pass and as soon as we enter the job market psychometric tests appear as an additional obstacle to getting the job we want.

For many of us the prospect of taking a test provokes anxiety, worry and even dread. In the days before the test session we fret about our ability to pass, stress about the experience of the testing session and possibly suffer very real physical reactions such as a racing heart or churning stomach.

Current graduates are probably the most tested generation in history. Not only have they endured a lifetime of academic testing, they are also the most likely candidates to be applying for jobs that feature the most stringent forms of assessment as part of the recruitment process. But with psychometrics becoming increasingly widespread across all types of jobs the rest of us are unlikely to remain entirely untouched by the experience of being tested.

The stakes are high when you are being tested by an employer. You need to demonstrate your potential to perform well in the job and differentiate yourself from others in terms of your abilities. You may be competing against other candidates with greater experience of being tested. You may feel that your verbal ability is not your strongest suit. You may hate taking tests, perhaps because of some unfortunate experiences in your past.

So there's a lot of fear and loathing mixed up in the whole testing process. But what can you do to develop an effective response? How can you ensure that your performance on a verbal test paints you in your best possible light?

If you work through this book you will develop the skills you need to practise and pass verbal tests. But a good point to start the process is to understand why employers use verbal tests and how verbal tests can help you – there is good news and reassurance to be enjoyed before you begin your journey.

WHY EMPLOYERS USE VERBAL TESTS

Test use in the UK is much more widespread than in many other parts of the world and reflects the degree to which the science of psychometrics is dominated by UK expertise. A 2009 survey conducted by the Chartered Institute of Personnel and Development (CIPD) found that of the 755 UK employers who participated in the survey, between 40% and 50% were using tests of ability. The proportion of this figure using verbal tests is likely to be very high since verbal ability is the most commonly tested form.

For the majority of employers using verbal tests, the main purpose of the test will be for recruitment. Employers have traditionally used verbal tests at the second stage of the recruitment process once they have sifted applications into a shortlist of candidates based on CVs and application form information. These shortlisted candidates are invited to visit the employer to take the test, typically on the same day as the interview. The information from the verbal test can then be used alongside the evidence gathered during the interview to make hiring decisions about the shortlist of candidates.

In recent years many employers have moved verbal tests further forward in the recruitment process to the first stage. This is a different approach where the verbal test is used as a 'pre-selection' assessment alongside the CV or application form. The difference for candidates is that everybody is tested when they apply for the job and the results from the test are used alongside the CV or application form information to make decisions about who will be shortlisted and invited for interview. If you are asked to complete a verbal test upfront when first applying for a job, the assessment will usually be completed online using a web-based verbal test. This means that you don't have to visit the employer to be tested. (Chapter 6 of this book provides specific advice about completing a verbal test online.)

INSIDER INFO

PREDICTING JOB PERFORMANCE

Ability tests have been found to be a strong predictor of performance at work compared to other assessment methods. Business psychologists investigate the power of different selection techniques by conducting 'validity studies' that compare scores gathered during a recruitment process with actual performance in the job.

The results of these studies show that there is a much higher correlation between an individual's verbal test score and their subsequent job performance than there is with other assessment techniques. In general, verbal tests predict job performance better than interviews, CVs and personality questionnaires.

Type of recruitment tool	Percentage of surveyed companies who use it
Competency-based interviews	69%
Interviews based on contents of a CV/ application form	68%
Panel interviews (more than one interviewer present)	59%
Specific ability tests	**50%**
General ability tests	44%
Literacy and/or numeracy tests (e.g. basic verbal ability test)	39%
Telephone interviews	38%
Personality questionnaires	35%
Assessment centres	35%
Group exercises (e.g. role-playing)	26%
Pre-interview referencing	19%
Online tests (selection)	17%
Other	6%

This figure of 50% in the CIPD survey seems more significant when compared with the proportion of these UK employers who use interviews as part of their selection processes (68%). So while the interview is still the most widely used method of recruitment, the use of ability tests is not too far behind. The table above shows the results of the survey in more detail.

So why do so many employers use tests and verbal ones in particular?

Many employers use verbal tests when selecting people for jobs. The tests help them to make accurate predictions about whether a person has the verbal aptitudes needed to succeed in a particular job. This information is difficult to assess through interview alone and is critical to performance in a wide range of jobs.

Verbal tests are also used by employers to help identify appropriate training and development for individuals at work. The test is used as a diagnostic tool and can provide objective information about people's strengths and limitations. This may be used to identify the development needs of the individual or establish their suitability for a training course or programme.

Verbal ability tests provide information that is less prone to bias and subjective judgement than other forms of assessment, such as interviews and CVs. A verbal ability test is a much fairer assessment since it presents all candidates with a level playing field and uses an objective scoring process. Employers

INSIDER INFO

WORK-PLACE TESTING – WHO'S TO BLAME?

If you want to blame anyone for verbal ability tests you could choose the Chinese, or more specifically the Chinese civil service in 50BC. This is the earliest recorded instance of testing being used in the workplace for recruitment purposes. To get a government job, candidates would have to study an official syllabus of civil service skills and knowledge and then complete an entrance test. Only those who passed the test could work for the government.

Methods have evolved since 50BC but this approach established the basic format for testing as part of recruitment.

therefore include verbal ability tests to increase the fairness and defensibility of their recruitment processes.

HOW VERBAL TESTS CAN WORK IN YOUR FAVOUR

Given the widespread use of tests by employers it is very likely that you will encounter a verbal test at some point in your career. There is some good news though – verbal tests can also be your friend because they offer you a number of benefits over traditional forms of recruitment such as the interview.

Verbal tests give you an opportunity to demonstrate aptitudes that are important for success, in a fair and objective context.

INSIDER INFO

WHAT'S MY IQ?

IQ (Intelligence Quotient) tests have existed for over a hundred years and were first developed for use within educational contexts to identify potential in children. The tests became controversial in the twentieth century with a number of researchers reporting differences in IQ scores between different racial groups. Today you are very unlikely to be asked to complete an IQ test at work.

A proper IQ test is completed in a one-to-one assessment that takes a few hours to complete. An average IQ score is 100 – around two-thirds of people score in this range. The highest score is 160 and the lowest 40, but only a tiny percentage of people score in these ranges.

Proponents of IQ tests argue that the IQ score indicates the intelligence of the individual. Many business psychologists question the link between IQ and intelligence, contending that IQ tests simply measure how good you are at IQ tests.

They may help you to show that you are the right person for a job. You can use verbal tests to identify areas in which you need to improve your verbal abilities. This can help to guide your career progression through the jobs you apply for or the self-development you undertake in your existing role. Verbal aptitudes which are actually used in jobs are tested using questions that are related to work. This means that you can use the experience of completing the verbal test to help you be sure that you pick a job that actually suits you, that you will do well in, and that you will gain satisfaction from.

CHAPTER 2
DEVELOPING YOUR PERSONAL BEST SCORE

Testing is nearly always high stakes – if you've been asked to take a verbal test it's generally to demonstrate that you have the right abilities for a job or training programme. When people fail tests it's often hard for them to understand how they could have performed at a level that would have got them the job or placement they wanted.

Sometimes people blame their luck or mood on the day of the test. When feeding back low test scores to others they will often say that their poor performance was the result of not being on top form on the day, or simply being unlucky with some of the answers they guessed.

Other people will blame the test itself – that the result is wrong and not a true reflection of their real verbal ability. Other people explain poor test results as being due to nerves, inexperience, confusion or ill-health. A few people attribute their low verbal test score to their low verbal ability.

In reality low test scores can be a combination of all these kinds of factors. And the good news is that you can do something about it.

WHERE DO LOW SCORES COME FROM?

Business psychologists work with people to help them develop their performance on tests and you can use these techniques to raise your own performance. Two people I have worked with in the past illustrate the different practise and pass approaches that are available to you.

Michael was a retail manager with many years experience running large departments within major supermarkets. He was asked to take a verbal reasoning test as part of a selection process for winning a place on a fast-track promotion programme into general store management jobs.

The verbal reasoning test formed part of the selection process, and while failing the test would not lead to an automatic rejection it would be a negative factor in the decision to award a place on the programme.

Michael felt reasonably confident about the verbal test since he often used the abilities it measured in his day-to-day job – writing management reports, understanding complex documents and making decisions based on emails, letters and policy documents. He was therefore surprised to learn that his test score was below average compared to other managers who had taken the test before (see Chapter 7 for an explanation of how test results like these are calculated). Michael did not win a place on the fast-track promotion programme on this occasion.

Louise was a new law graduate who had recently completed a summer internship at a large law firm. She applied to the law firm's graduate training programme to join the firm as a full-time employee. The initial part of the recruitment process was an online verbal critical-reasoning test. On her initial application Louise failed to score at a level that formed the pass-mark for invitation to interview.

While she was disappointed Louise took action to improve her score for her second attempt six months later, and completed a huge number of verbal test practice questions. At the second attempt her score moved up a few points but still failed to achieve the pass-mark.

Both Michael and Louise were understandably frustrated – Michael because he felt that his verbal test score did not reflect his real abilities and Louise because of her test score's stubborn refusal to improve much despite all the practice she had put in over the six months.

In helping Michael and Louise to practise and pass their verbal tests I encouraged them to refocus their efforts on **achieving their personal best** verbal test scores.

WHAT IS YOUR PERSONAL BEST?

Your personal best score is the maximum you can hope to achieve on a specific type of test. To achieve your personal best score you must tackle all of the causes of low test scores. These causes fall into three broad categories:

- ▶ Lack of knowledge
- ▶ Lack of strategy
- ▶ Lack of practice

Michael had a relatively high level of verbal ability but this was not reflected in his test score. He failed to score his personal best verbal test result because of a lack of knowledge and strategy. This led him to be a poor test-taker – he lacked understanding of how the test worked and the best approach to take during the test session. His well practised and developed verbal ability was let down by his inexperience and poor test-taking strategy.

Louise completed a lot of verbal practice questions, which improved her test score a little. She still failed to achieve her personal best score as a result of poor test-taking strategy and a narrow range of practice.

To help them achieve their personal best verbal test scores I helped them address the causes of their low scores by making improvements in the areas that were holding them back. As a result Michael went on to win a place on the promotion

INSIDER INFO

THE SCIENCE OF PSYCHOMETRICS – YOUR PERSONAL BEST SCORE

The term 'personal best score' is drawn from classical test theory. This is a model used by business psychologists in the development of ability tests to interpret candidate results. Classical test theory states that for any given test people have a true-score of ability. This true score perfectly represents the individual's ability on that test.

For example, you have a true score which represents your verbal ability. The challenge for test developers is to ensure that the verbal ability test accurately measures your verbal true score. Verbal tests that are badly designed or poorly administered introduce error into the measurement of your true score. This distorts the measurement of your verbal ability; the test no longer accurately measures the real level of your ability – your personal best.

The challenge for you as a test-taker is to make sure that you demonstrate your true score when you take the test. If you are ill-prepared, unpractised or have poor test-taking strategies you will not demonstrate your true score no matter how well designed the test.

programme and Louise made it through to the next round of the interview process.

You can use the same techniques to practise and pass verbal tests by following the three steps for developing your personal best score.

THE THREE STEPS FOR DEVELOPING YOUR PERSONAL BEST

Achieving your personal best score means addressing all of the possible causes of a low test score.

- ▶ You must increase your **knowledge** of the test so that you understand how it works.
- ▶ You must develop your test-taking **strategies** so that you are not let down by a poor performance on the day.
- ▶ You must **practise** in order to develop your verbal ability to its maximum possible level.

STEP 1: KNOWLEDGE – KNOW YOUR ENEMY!

The first step to achieving your personal best score on a verbal test is to understand what a verbal reasoning test is and how it works. If you are unprepared in terms of your knowledge of the test you are unlikely to demonstrate your maximum level of ability.

This section will help you to develop your knowledge of verbal tests and enable you to arrive at the test session well prepared and ready to demonstrate your best. You can take your preparation further by finding out more about the specific verbal test you are due to complete. (See the section 'Find out more about your specific test' later in this chapter for more advice.)

Verbal tests and the demands of the job

Employers use verbal ability tests because they provide information about your aptitude or potential for performing well at certain critical demands of the job. You use verbal ability to perform effectively at a range of tasks such as:

▸ Understanding safety warnings
▸ Learning from training materials
▸ Analysing complex documents
▸ Understanding emails, letters and reports
▸ Solving complex problems
▸ Applying rules, procedures and processes correctly
▸ Making decisions based on written information
▸ Applying abstract reasoning or lateral thinking
▸ Composing letters, reports or written arguments
▸ Understanding what other people are saying
▸ Contributing effectively to discussions

Verbal tests measure abilities that are central to much of what people do in the vast majority of jobs, which is why they are one of the most commonly used types of tests. You can therefore gauge the level of demands within the job from the level of difficulty of the test.

Verbal tests are often used alongside other types of test within a recruitment or training process, such as a numerical test. This can be a reflection of the wide range of abilities required for effective performance in a job or sometimes employers are interested in understanding your general ability by asking you to complete more than one type of test. If you are asked to complete a verbal test as part of a job application it is very likely that you will also be asked to complete an additional test of ability, and the most likely choice is a numerical test. Remember that you need to focus time on developing your numerical score as well as your verbal score. You could do this using the *Practice & Pass Professional: Numeracy Tests* book that is also part of this series.

How verbal tests work

Modern verbal tests used as part of recruitment and training processes measure your ability to read, comprehend and make decisions based on written information. Verbal tests require you to read a passage of written information and then answer a series of questions relating to the information you have read.

Each question is in the form of a statement and usually your job is to decide whether the statement is true or false in relation to the information. Here's a typical example, which is based on information in the previous paragraph:

'Verbal tests are sometimes used in recruitment processes. True or false?'

The correct answer to that question is *True* – you can see from the information provided that modern verbal tests are used as part of recruitment processes. The key to answering the question correctly is to have read the passage and only use the information provided to answer the question – rather than rely on any other information you might already know about verbal tests.

INSIDER INFO

INTELLIGENCE AND GENERAL ABILITY

The term 'general ability' is used by many psychologists to describe the intelligence of the individual. Early IQ tests were developed to measure general ability and would include a verbal test alongside other tests, such as abstract reasoning, sequential ability and spatial reasoning. The test developers believed that the way to measure intelligence was to assess lots of smaller, specific abilities in this way and then add their scores together. The overall score (such as an IQ) would describe general ability across a range of tests and therefore indicate intelligence.

Modern employers often adopt a similar approach by using one or two different ability tests, such as verbal and numerical, and then combining the scores to understand the individual's overall ability.

Multiple-choice answers

Verbal tests using this type of approach will also use a multiple-choice format for giving your answers. Sometimes there are just two options to choose from: **true** or **false**. More advanced verbal tests will have three options: **true**, **false** or **cannot say**. The cannot say option is used when we cannot say for certain from the information given whether the statement is true or false. (The cannot say option does not mean 'I don't know'!)

Here's another example based on the same paragraph:

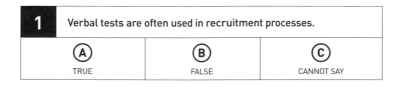

1	Verbal tests are often used in recruitment processes.	
Ⓐ TRUE	Ⓑ FALSE	Ⓒ CANNOT SAY

The correct answer is C: cannot say. The key to answering this question correctly is to focus on what the passage says. The information tells us that verbal tests are used in recruitment but there is no indication of how frequently they are used. It is impossible to say from the information given whether the statement is true or false – so the correct answer is cannot say. Remember, 'cannot say' is not the same as 'don't know'.

Older question formats

If you are asked to complete an older verbal ability test you may find that the question format differs from the multiple-choice approach used in modern tests. These more traditional formats are based on tests used in education. One example is a passage of verbal information followed by a series of statements, from which you have to identify the true statement. Here's an example:

'Modern verbal tests used as part of recruitment and training processes measure your ability to read, comprehend and make decisions based on written information. Verbal tests require you to read a passage of written information and then answer a series of questions relating to the information you have read.'

Which of these statements is true according to the information given?

A: Verbal tests are often used in recruitment processes.

B: Verbal tests measure your ability to perform calculations.

C: Verbal tests contain a series of questions based on a passage of information.

D: Verbal tests are used by many employers for recruitment purposes.

The correct answer is statement C, because it is true according to the information given.

This approach does not tend to appear in modern, occupational tests of verbal ability and if you are given a test that uses this format it is likely that the employer has chosen to use an out-of-date test.

The good news for you as a test taker is that the approach that you take to practise and pass modern verbal ability tests works for this old-fashioned format as well. The decision-making processes you use to decide whether a statement is true, false, or cannot say can be applied directly to questions using this more traditional format. This approach is described in Chapters 3, 4 and 5.

If we apply this approach to the question above we can see that in relation to the information:

▶ Statement A is Cannot say
▶ Statement B is False
▶ Statement C is True (and therefore the correct answer in this example)
▶ Statement D is Cannot say

As modern test designers, we tend to adopt the true, false, cannot say approach since it enables us to design tests that place a range of demands on the verbal abilities of test-takers. In a modern verbal test, statements A, B, C and D in the example above would appear as separate questions, each using the true, false, cannot say multiple-choice answer format.

An even older question format

Very traditional verbal tests sometimes use a format like this:

'Modern verbal tests used as part of recruitment and training processes measure your ability to read, comprehend and make decisions based on written information. Verbal tests require you to read a passage of written information and then answer a series of questions relating to the information you have read.'

Complete this statement from the four choices below:

Verbal tests are to your verbal ability as a tape measure is to...

A: your weight

B: your tool-kit

C: a set of bathroom scales

D: your height

The correct answer to this verbal test question is statement D – a tape measure provides a measurement of your height in the same way that a verbal test provides a measurement of your verbal ability.

Modern test developers often avoid this question format because it tends to use language and examples from outside the workplace, which may confuse some groups, and it measures a very narrow aspect of your verbal ability.

Again, if you see this question format you can make the assumption that the employer has chosen to use a more old-fashioned test, which might reflect their more general style as an employer. In terms of practising and passing verbal tests, the work that you complete within this book will help you develop the underlying verbal ability that you will need to answer this old question format correctly.

There are other types of verbal test and question format that are not used in contemporary verbal test design. These are described later in this chapter, along with other myths about verbal tests.

Timing

Verbal tests usually have a strict time limit within which you must answer the questions. The questions that you answer within this time form the basis of your score for the test, which is typically based on a calculation that compares your number of correct answers with an average for that test. Some tests are designed to give you plenty of time to answer all of the questions while others use a very tight time limit, which means you are unlikely to answer all the questions before the test ends. In both cases you should work quickly but accurately.

Go to the section 'Step 2: Strategies' later in this chapter for more information about how tests are timed.

Go to Chapter 3 for more advice on how to answer verbal test questions correctly.

Go to Chapter 7 for more detail on how tests are scored and what the results mean.

Different levels of verbal testing

Employers should ask you to complete a verbal test that reflects the demands of the job and the level of difficulty of those demands. Verbal tests are pitched at three levels of difficulty.

1. Verbal comprehension.
2. Verbal reasoning.
3. Verbal critical reasoning.

The main focus of this book is on levels 2 and 3 because these are the most frequently tested types of verbal ability. You will still find it valuable to work through the level 1 practice questions in the book because these can help you to polish the foundations of your verbal test performance.

Verbal comprehension tests

Verbal comprehension tests are the simplest form of verbal ability test. They are based on clear and straightforward verbal information and a series of true/false questions.

The questions are designed to assess your understanding of the verbal information. You are not required to make decisions or solve complex problems during the test. Your job is to demonstrate that you can read and understand the level of written information that you would encounter in the job itself.

Verbal comprehension tests are generally used in recruitment and training processes for jobs that do not require high levels of verbal ability. The tests are used to determine whether you have the minimum level of verbal ability to deal with the written information in the job. For example, a verbal comprehension test may be used in the recruitment process for production workers in a car factory. This job requires many complex skills but only requires verbal ability at a basic level. The employer in this case would use the verbal test to confirm that you would be able to read safety warnings and understand training materials in the job.

You can easily spot a verbal comprehension test by the true/false multiple choice format. When a test includes a cannot say option it is more likely to be pitched at a higher level of difficulty.

Go to Chapter 3 for practice questions and advice on the best approach to taking a verbal comprehension test.

Verbal reasoning tests

Verbal reasoning tests are the most widely used form of verbal ability test because they reflect the level of demands in the majority of jobs. The written information in these tests is likely to be more complex than the content of a verbal comprehension test. The multiple choice format will include a cannot say option.

A verbal reasoning test measures a more advanced type of verbal ability. Not only are you required to read and understand the written information, you also need to reason with it. This means you must make decisions based on what you understand the information to mean. The cannot say answer option introduces an additional element of complexity to the more simple true/false approach used in easier verbal tests.

Verbal reasoning tests are generally used in recruitment and training processes for jobs that require mid-levels of verbal ability. The tests are used with a broad range of educational levels, from school leavers to graduate level candidates. The broad nature of the ability measured by verbal reasoning tests means that the questions within the test vary a great deal in difficulty, and there are likely to be some questions you find harder than others to answer.

Verbal reasoning tests are used to assess your potential to deal effectively with a wide range of job demands. For example, a verbal reasoning test may be used in the recruitment process for call centre staff. This job requires important attributes such as customer service skills but also requires you to demonstrate a level of verbal ability that is sufficient to deal with the more complex aspects of the role. The employer in this example would use the verbal reasoning test to confirm that you would be able to learn to follow systems and procedures correctly, problem-solve effectively and understand complex customer service issues.

Go to Chapter 4 for practice questions and advice on taking a verbal reasoning test.

Verbal critical-reasoning tests

Verbal critical-reasoning tests are the most advanced form of verbal test. These tests contain complex and high-level verbal information that is designed to simulate the demands of senior level jobs.

The questions are designed to assess your ability to draw conclusions and make complex decisions about the verbal information in the test. These decisions sometimes require you to use inference or deal with ambiguity in the information. Sometimes it is the sheer complexity of the written information that requires high levels of verbal ability to answer the questions correctly. The cannot say multiple choice answer option is included to further increase the demands of the test.

Verbal critical-reasoning tests are used in recruitment and training processes for jobs that require the highest levels of

INSIDER INFO

BESPOKE AND SPECIALIST VERBAL TESTS

Verbal tests tend to be fairly generic across different types of jobs or sectors, so verbal tests used for any role, including more technical jobs in finance or IT, will generally be identical. Employers buy off-the-shelf tests from test publishers and this is why you will sometimes be asked to take the same test by different organisations.

Some employers will ask business psychologists to develop bespoke tests for the organisation. I have developed bespoke verbal tests for a range of larger organisations over the years that are based on verbal material specific to each job or organisation.

When developing bespoke or specialist tests we ensure that you do not need prior knowledge of the specific role or business to do well. We also make sure that the verbal content of the test is very representative of real demands in the job, which gives you the test-taker a valuable insight into whether or not it's the right job for you.

For jobs in areas like IT or finance, employers will often use verbal tests alongside other types of test, such as numerical critical reasoning or abstract reasoning.

verbal ability. The tests are used to determine whether you have the mental firepower to deal with the complex nature of the job. For example, a verbal critical-reasoning test may be used in the recruitment process for lawyers, a job that requires verbal abilities of sufficient power to understand complex information, solve difficult problems and make demanding decisions.

Go to Chapter 5 for practice questions and advice on passing verbal critical-reasoning tests.

Verbal test materials

A valuable piece of preparation for taking a verbal test is to ensure that you are familiar with the format of the materials you will use to complete the test. Most modern verbal tests follow a similar approach to the format of the 'paper and pencil' test materials. When you complete the test you will be given everything you need, which should include:

- ▶ A test booklet – this contains the instructions for taking the test and the test pages themselves with written information and questions. You should not write on this booklet as it is designed to be reusable
- ▶ An answer sheet – this is what you use to record your answers
- ▶ Pencil and eraser or a pen

People who have not taken many tests in the past sometimes find the plethora of test materials confusing. If you can prepare by familiarising yourself with knowledge of the format of the test materials you will be less likely to become confused or flustered in the heat of the testing session.

Most paper and pencil verbal test materials follow the format described here. You can take your preparation further by finding out more about the specific verbal test you are due to complete.

You may be asked to complete a verbal test via the internet. Online tests follow a different format to traditional paper and pencil tests.

Go to the section 'Find out more about your specific test' later in this chapter for more information.

Go to Chapter 6 to find out more about online testing.

Some myths about verbal tests

Even those of us who left school many years ago may still have memories of verbal tests we were asked to complete

INSIDER INFO

OLD-SCHOOL VERBAL TESTS

Modern occupational tests have their roots in older educational tests. In fact very early occupational tests of ability look a lot like their educational forebears. If you are asked to complete an ability test that looks and feels like an old school test you may form the impression that the potential employer is a bit old fashioned, and has not updated their recruitment processes for many years. The test itself may be outdated and the results somewhat questionable.

Modern, professional employers seek to use contemporary verbal tests that reflect the style and demands of their workplace. If you are asked to complete an old fashioned looking test it might be because the employer itself is somewhat old school – this might influence your decision about whether or not the job is right for you.

during our education. Sometimes these were vocabulary tests, spelling tests or comprehension tests. For most people educational testing is the first experience of being tested.

To practise and pass a verbal test for an employer you need to let go of any preconceptions that you have about testing based on your experiences at school. Modern tests that have been designed to be used in a workplace have little in common with those used in schools. There are a number of myths about testing that are based on educational experiences.

Verbal tests you'll never see in real life

Modern employers do not use verbal tests that are based on school-like formats such as:

▸ Sentence completion
▸ Word substitution

INSIDER INFO

INAPPROPRIATE TESTING

There are employment law implications for using tests that contain inappropriate content. In order to be a fair assessment of your suitability to do the job the test must contain tasks and demands that reflect the content of the job.

Employers tend to avoid tests that contain school-like content because they do not match the content of the job. Modern verbal tests reflect occupational life very closely.

Employers use tests that contain content like sentence completion or word association at their peril. If they are ever challenged over the fairness of a recruitment decision their use of such tests would be hard to defend.

- ▶ Vocabulary
- ▶ Spelling
- ▶ Word association
- ▶ Missing words
- ▶ Word pairs

These formats have fallen out of favour with employers because they rely too heavily on learned information – such as your command of English. They do not measure your raw verbal ability in a way that is fair to all candidates from all backgrounds.

Verbal tests that you are asked to complete for an employer should be based on everyday, business-related information, which you use to correctly answer questions following a true/false/cannot say multiple-choice format.

Revision for tests

You cannot revise for a verbal ability test. Modern tests require no prior knowledge and so you can't revise for them in the same way that you do a school exam. You can prepare for verbal tests – which is why you're reading this book!

No long-hand written answers

Modern verbal tests do not require you to write long essay-style answers like school exams. Verbal tests use a multiple-choice format to make scoring easy and fair.

No memory testing

You are not required to memorise the written information used in a verbal test. You can refer to the information in the test booklet to answer the questions throughout the test session.

Some newer verbal tests even give you reading time before the test begins to enable you to familiarise yourself with the written information.

INSIDER INFO

BIAS IN TESTING

Modern tests have to perform against stringent standards of fairness. All candidates regardless of background should have an equal chance to perform well on the test. Early tests were often biased against certain groups. IQ tests became controversial because some groups of people scored higher than others – white, middle-class men being the highest scoring group. This led a number of psychologists to incorrectly believe that there were real differences in IQ between groups – in fact it was simply the result of bias in the test.

Modern tests are developed to minimise such bias by ensuring that the cultural, educational, and social background of candidates does not confer an advantage or disadvantage.

No marks taken off for wrong answers

Contemporary verbal ability tests do not take marks of for wrong answers. This is an approach sometimes used by old-fashioned educational tests to try to compensate for people guessing the correct answers. By taking points away for wrong answers educational testers believed they would deter guessing.

The scoring process for modern, occupational verbal tests is kept secret by the test developers to prevent cheating and there may be a correction made to test scores to compensate for possible guessing, but modern tests do not subtract scores for answering incorrectly.

Find out more about your specific test

Your knowledge of verbal tests will ensure that you are better prepared for the testing session. By letting go of any testing myths and understanding the format and materials of verbal tests you will be in a much better position to benefit from your efforts to practise and develop your test-taking strategies.

You can develop your knowledge further by finding out more about the specific test you will be taking. This will ensure that you are prepared to deal with anything unusual or idiosyncratic about the precise test you are asked to complete. Some of the sources of information you could try are given below.

Ask the employer

The organisation that has asked you to complete the test should provide you with details about the specific assessment they use. It is part of the testing best-practice code for employers to ensure that their test candidates are fully informed about the testing process.

Test practice materials

Test publishers offer practice materials for the tests they provide to employers. These practice materials build on the information and advice in this book by providing guidance and example questions specific to the test you will take. While it is not compulsory for employers to send practice materials to their test candidates, it is best practice.

If the employer who has asked you to complete the verbal test has not provided any practice materials prior to testing you could contact them to find out who publishes the test they will be using. You can then contact this test publisher for advice about the test. Many test publishers provide free practice materials specific to their tests.

Go to Chapter 9 for a list of test publishers who provide practice questions on their websites.

British Psychological Society (BPS)

Visit the BPS website (www.psychtesting.org.uk) for advice to candidates taking a test.

Go to Chapter 9 for details on the other resources that are out there.

STEP 2: STRATEGIES – LEVELLING THE PLAYING FIELD

The second step to achieving your personal best score on a verbal test is to develop your test-taking strategies. Your approach during the test session can make a big difference to your test score. Candidates who have poor test-taking strategies are much less likely to achieve their personal best score – regardless of their knowledge of the test and the practice they have done. If you are unprepared in terms of your test-taking strategies then you are unlikely to demonstrate your maximum level of ability.

How test strategies can help you

Experienced test-takers tend to have high levels of test-sophistication – they know the best approach to take during the test session. Taking lots of tests gives them an advantage over less experienced candidates because of the strategies and techniques they have developed though their exposure to tests.

You can level the playing field by developing these test-taking strategies yourself. This will enable you to compete with the most experienced test-takers and maximise your own score. Research into test performance has shown that increased test-sophistication can lead to significant increases in test scores. The more valuable test-taking strategies demonstrated by test-sophisticated candidates are described below.

Before the test session

Make sure that you are in peak form for completing the test. Get a good night's sleep the evening before the session. Arrive at the testing location in plenty of time – you don't want the stress of a delay distracting you from performing at your best. If you need spectacles for reading you will need them for the test.

Listen very carefully

The test administrator will read aloud from a test administration card, and you will be asked to read the instructions from your test booklet at the same time. Make sure you focus on what the administrator tells you – do not let your mind wander to try to read ahead to the later stages of the instructions or you may miss something important.

Ask questions

If there is anything that you do not understand, make sure you ask about it before you start the test. Do not feel nervous about asking questions – you can avoid making silly mistakes by making sure you completely understand what you need to do during the test. In most test sessions you are not allowed to ask questions once the timed part of the test has begun, so make sure you clear up any uncertainties you have in the beginning part of the test session.

Pace yourself

Make sure you know how much time you have for the tests so that you can pace yourself. Most sessions do not have any reminders or warnings about the amount of time you have left. You can write a note of the time that you started the test on your answer sheet or any rough paper you've been given so that you do not forget. For tests that look like power tests (generous time limit for the number of questions) you should not set yourself a time limit for each question because some will be harder than others. For speed tests (short time limit for the total number of questions) you need to work quickly but accurately – but do not expect to finish them all.

Concentrate

Work as quickly and accurately as you can and do not get distracted. Do not be worried by what other candidates are doing. Focus on your own performance. If you're completing the test online remotely try to use a quiet location free from distractions.

Do not get stuck

If you find a particular question difficult do not spend too much time on it. Leave it and go on to the next. If you have time you can always come back to it at the end. You should not leave any questions blank once you have completed the test, so make a note of any questions that you have left unanswered so that you can return to them at the end of the test (before the time limit for the test is reached).

Avoid guessing

When you are not sure of an answer do not simply guess randomly. Try and narrow down the options by deciding which of the answers, true, false or cannot say, is most likely to be incorrect. From the two remaining options try and identify which is the most likely to be correct. It is better to use this 'best guess' than leave a question blank.

Revisit your answers

If you complete all the questions before the end of the time limit use the time you have left to revisit and check your answers. Focus particularly on questions where you struggled or had to give your best guess.

Speed vs power

Some tests are speeded – they have a short time limit and a lot of questions; candidates are not expected to attempt all the questions within a speed test. Other verbal tests are power tests – they have a more generous time limit for the total number of questions and are designed to enable the vast majority of candidates to attempt all the questions within the time available.

You can identify whether a verbal test is a speed or power test by applying a rule of thumb to the number of questions in the test compared with the time limit. If you are allowed less than 20 seconds per question then it is more likely to be a speed test.

You should adjust your test-taking strategy depending on whether the test looks like a speed or power test. With power tests the questions are likely to become more difficult as the test progresses, but you are likely to have time to attempt all the questions in the test. This means that you should adjust your test-taking strategy for a power test in the following ways.

The power test

▶ **Pace yourself.** You do not need to rush but you shouldn't dwell too long on any question where you become stuck. Leave the question until you have attempted all the other questions in the test – you are likely to have sufficient time at the end to return to the question and try again. Many people find that leaving a question helps clear their thinking, which makes the answer more obvious when they come back to try again. Perhaps your unconscious carries on working on the question in the background while your rational mind focuses on the other questions you work on?

▶ **Expect to slow down.** As the questions become harder your pace will decrease. This is normal so you should allow yourself more time for the questions you find more difficult as you get towards the end of the test. Do not try and maintain the same pace throughout the test.

▶ **Use any extra time well.** The more generous time-limits of a power test mean that you are more likely to have some time left over at the end once you've attempted all the questions than you would for a speed test. Use this time well to check your answers and revisit any questions you struggled with initially.

The speed test

Speed tests require a different focus for your test-taking
strategies. With a speeded verbal test you are much less likely
to have time to attempt all the questions in the test and much
more likely to run out of time before you finish. The questions
themselves are less likely to increase in difficulty in the same
way that the questions in a power test do. These features of
a speed test mean that you need to adjust your test taking
strategy in the following ways.

▶ **Pace yourself.** Your score on a verbal speed test will
  be heavily influenced by the number of questions you
  manage to answer in the time available. But you also
  need to answer the questions correctly – there are no
  marks for wrong answers no matter how many you
  answer within the time limit. This means that you have
  to pace yourself effectively. The most serious mistake
  to avoid is spending too long on a question that you get
  stuck with. Do not waste precious minutes struggling
  with a question – you could be using this time to answer
  other questions correctly and pushing up your test
  score. If you do not know the answer to a question you
  should apply the usual test-taking strategy of giving the
  answer you think is best without simply guessing as
  described in the earlier section on avoiding guessing.

▶ **Don't panic.** Some people feel under additional
  pressure when taking a speed test because of the
  sense of the insufficient time period ticking away in the
  background. This is bad news if the panic affects your
  concentration and ability to answer questions correctly.
  Remind yourself that the time-limit is part of the test
  and therefore affects everybody who takes the test.

You are not expected to attempt all the questions in the test and you should not try to. Instead you should focus on calming yourself and concentrating on the task at hand, which is answering each test question in turn. (Go to the section 'Calming and focusing strategies' below for advice on managing your emotions.)

▶ **Don't cheat!** Some people are very tempted to use the closing seconds of the time-limit to quickly fill in the answers to questions that they have not yet attempted. The temptation is understandable; if the multiple choices are true, false and cannot say then you would have a 1 in 3 chance of guessing each question correctly. Be aware though that the scoring mechanism for tests can include a correction for this type of test-taking behaviour which would adversely affect your test result. The cost of randomly guessing some questions at the end of the time-limit could be a worse test result than if you'd simply let things be and had your score based purely on the questions you attempted legitimately.

Whether a test is a speed one or a power one your main focus should still be on answering the questions correctly – this is, after all, what drives your verbal test score. Do not worry and fret after the test if you did not answer all the questions or you are unsure of some of your answers. The scoring and time limits of verbal tests are carefully designed to ensure an accurate measurement of your verbal ability. The number of questions you attempted correctly is a reflection of the design of the test and your level of verbal ability. Provided you applied the appropriate test-taking strategies your performance should reflect your personal best score.

INSIDER INFO

SPEED TESTS VS. POWER TESTS

Tests with a generous time-limit are called **power tests**. They are designed to measure the power of your verbal ability – in other words they establish the maximum level of difficulty you can perform at. A power test is designed so that most people have enough time to answer all the questions before the end of the test, but the questions get progressively more difficult as you complete the test – the final questions are much harder than the early ones.

Speed tests set a very tight time-limit – they are not designed to enable you to complete all the questions before the test ends. These tests measure the speed of your verbal ability – how quickly you can answer questions of equal difficulty. The questions do not become harder as you progress.

A typical verbal ability speed test might have 40 questions but only a 10-minute time-limit, while a verbal ability power test might have 30 questions and a 20-minute time-limit. You can determine whether a test is more speed or more power by looking at this ratio of number of questions to amount of time allowed. If the test allows less than 20 seconds per question it is more likely to be a speed test.

Calming and focusing strategies

In addition to developing your test sophistication through the strategies you adopt during the test session it is important to make sure that your emotional and mental states are focused on achieving your personal best score.

Prior to the test session you should spend some time preparing your mind and emotions. To perform at your best during the test session you need to feel calm, focused and at your mental peak.

Many people feel anxious before and during a test session, especially when there is a lot riding on the results. You need to deal with these nerves to prevent them from affecting your performance. You can draw from the techniques described below, which are often used by sports psychologists when helping athletes to reach their peak performance.

Centre your breathing

Prior to and during the test session you can centre yourself and minimise any nerves by focusing your attention entirely on your breathing. Still your mind and quieten worries by simply extending your breaths and using the full extent of your lungs. Try to make each breath softer and longer than the last.

Look at the trees

Before attempting a challenge sportspeople will often 'look at the trees'; they take a moment away from the immediate situation and its demands and look into the distance. You do not need to be near any trees or even outside – simply take a moment to gaze into the middle-distance before embarking on the challenge.

Focus on your objectives

Both centring your breathing and 'looking at the trees' provide you with a valuable opportunity to focus on your objectives. In that moment of calm you should remind yourself what you are here to do. Do not allow your mind to worry about the outcome; instead rehearse in your mind what you are going to do during the test session.

Remember a calm place

Remove your mind from the stress of the situation by bringing to mind a place where you have felt calm. This does not have to be a real place but you need to be able to imagine it in as much detail as possible. Distract your mind from the worries taking up space by running through each of your senses – remember how the calm place looks, feels, smells and sounds.

Name your feelings

Focus your attention on the physical sensations of your body. Notice any feelings that the anxiety is causing. Explore each part of your body and note any tension, discomfort, heat or any other sensations. Each time you discover a symptom you should spend some time breathing it away.

Get some help

If your test nerves are extreme then you could consider seeking some professional help. Many people have found hypnotherapy a useful aid to controlling nerves and anxiety in pressured

INSIDER INFO

SUPERVISED VS. REMOTE TESTING

Traditional testing follows the format of examinations – though candidates are tested in smaller groups by a test administrator rather than an invigilator.

Online tests are often administered remotely. This removes the need for candidates to visit the testing centre and saves time for the employer. The downside is that the testing is unsupervised and less standardised.

Go to Chapter 6 for more information and advice about online testing.

situations like tests, exams and interviews. A qualified hypnotherapist will be able to teach you techniques to get your feelings under control and focus your energies on maximising your performance.

Test session survival strategies

Tests are generally administered to small groups of candidates at the employer's offices. Online tests are usually administered remotely – in other words you complete them at home or at your office in your own time. (See Chapter 6 for more information about online testing.)

A traditional, supervised testing session can be stressful – not least because for many people it is an unfamiliar and confusing process.

Most testing sessions follow a similar structure that is designed to standardise the way in which tests are administered. This

INSIDER INFO

THE TEST ADMINISTRATOR

Test administration is a skilled job and requires specialist training. Anybody involved in the use of ability tests should be properly trained to administer and score the test. You can check the testing qualifications held by an employer by contacting the British Psychological Society's Psychological Testing Centre (see Chapter 9).

The test administrator's responsibilities are to ensure that the test session is as standardised as possible – in other words each session is identical to the last. The test administrator must also ensure that every candidate is able to perform at their best and not affected by nerves or a lack of understanding about the test.

standardised structure ensures testing is fair by introducing consistency across all test sessions – everyone who takes the test will experience the same conditions.

By understanding this structure you can combat many of the nerves associated with testing. You can also ensure that your results benefit from the elements of the testing structure that are designed to help you.

The test session structure

The testing session will be delivered by a trained test administrator who will follow a carefully defined set of steps for the specific test they are using.

▶ **Introduction** The test administrator will set the scene and tell you more about the test session. You should use this part of the process to ask any questions you have about the test. Remember that asking questions when uncertain is a key test-taking strategy.

▶ **Instructions** The test administrator will read the test instructions aloud from a card. These instructions will

INSIDER INFO

TEST SECURITY

Test administrators will collect all the materials before you are allowed to leave the testing room. This is to maintain the security of the test materials and to prevent them from being circulated among future candidates. Even rough paper is collected – candidates have been known to write the test questions and answers down to share with their friends.

be reproduced in your test booklet and you should read along when asked to do so. Clear your mind and read carefully to ensure you do not miss any details that are important. Avoid reading ahead or allowing your mind to wander. Remember that paying attention and focusing are key test-taking strategies. You can still ask questions at this stage of the process.

▸ **Example questions** At the end of the instructions the test administrator will ask you to complete some example questions. These do not contribute to your test score and they are not timed. They are designed to help you understand the format of the test. You can ask questions during this part of the process. If you have any difficulty with an example question the test administrator can help you to find the correct answer. Do not be worried if you answer an example question incorrectly – many people do because the questions are often designed to illustrate any tricky or complex aspect of the testing format (such as how the cannot say option works).

▸ **Before you begin** After the example questions the test administrator will read the final part of the test instructions from the card. This will include advice about how to do well during the test as well as remind you about the time-limit. This is your last chance to ask any questions.

▸ **Take the test** The test administrator will tell you to begin the test and will start the timer. You are not allowed to ask questions once the test has begun. The administrator may not alert you before the time is up so remember to make a note of the time you started.

INSIDER INFO

THE TEST LOG

Test administrators will record any unusual behaviour or events that they observe during the test session. Sometimes this might be information relating to the conditions of the test session – for example, if a car alarm was going off during the test. They will also record candidate behaviours, such as attempts to complete questions after the time limit. Any information recorded by the test administrator may be used to guide the interpretation of the test results for an individual candidate or the whole group.

▶ **Time's up** The test administrator will ask you to stop when the time-limit has been reached. The test administrator will collect all the test materials before thanking you and inviting you to move on to your next activity.

STEP 3: PRACTICE – DOESN'T MAKE PERFECT (ON ITS OWN)

The third and final step to achieving your personal best score on a verbal test is to practise. Remember that practice alone is not enough to perfect your test score – you also need to devote time to building your knowledge of the test and developing your test-taking strategies.

With knowledge and strategies in place your practice will reap you the maximum reward in terms of your test score. This combined approach is critical to achieving your personal best score.

INSIDER INFO

TAKING A TEST MORE THAN ONCE

Research conducted in the early 1990s identified the existence of 'practice effects' – the factors that affect people's test scores when they take the same test more than once. This can sometimes be a problem for test developers and employers when they are testing candidates who are applying to lots of other employers who all use the same test. Employers worry that people's test scores will increase because they remember the test and its questions from previous attempts. Some test publishers are keen to downplay the likelihood of a change in test scores following repeat administrations.

The research, which focused on graduates (who are the most frequently tested and retested group), found that people's test scores do tend to change when they take the same test twice. Many people's scores increase, but some stay the same and some decrease. The research ruled out the influence of memory and instead identified motivation, confidence and test sophistication as the key factors behind practice effects.

This can help you as a candidate. You will benefit from practice effects if you take tests repeatedly or work through this book, because you will develop confidence and test sophistication. To avoid a decrease in your test score you must maintain your motivation – do not become complacent or careless when taking a test no matter how confident you feel.

While practice effects happen with all types of test, this study found that numerical test results saw some of the biggest increases due to practice effects. If you are asked to complete a numerical test you can make big improvements to your personal best score by working through the *Practise & Pass Professional: Numeracy Tests* book.

What kind of practice helps?

The best type of practice is to complete example questions that are very similar to those in the specific test you will be taking.

The employer who asks you to complete a test may provide you with some example questions developed by the test publisher who built the specific verbal test you will be completing.

The practice questions in this book are another valuable resource. Unlike many verbal reasoning test books out there, these questions follow the same format as the questions you will find within modern verbal tests. Whether you use these in conjunction with example questions provided by the employer or as an alternative, these practice questions will enhance your ability to perform well in the test.

Practice questions help you improve your score in three ways.

▶ Completing the questions increases your knowledge of the test format.
▶ Advice on how to answer the practice questions correctly helps you refine your test-taking strategies.
▶ Completing the questions can help you develop the underlying ability measured by the test – answering verbal test questions can help you develop your verbal ability.

The practice questions in this book cover the levels of difficulty of different verbal tests. Working through these questions will help you develop your personal best test score.

Developing your raw verbal ability

There are additional forms of practice that can help you to develop your personal best score. Your verbal ability is like a muscle – and like any muscle it responds to exercise.

Regularly exercising your verbal ability will help it to grow and become stronger. If you do not exercise your ability, it will become weaker.

Completing practice questions will help you to exercise and therefore develop your verbal ability, but the benefits are limited. To build your raw ability to its maximum strength you need to combine the practising you complete with regular use of the ability. Practice combined with regular exercise will encourage your verbal ability to become stronger and well-rounded.

Your raw verbal ability can be exercised and developed through any activity that requires you to use it. Activities include:

- ▶ Completing crossword puzzles, word games, problem-solving challenges
- ▶ Reading – the more complex the material the better
- ▶ Learning – read material that requires you to develop knowledge or skills
- ▶ Analysis – read a complex passage and then spend some time analysing it. Identify key themes or points or look for underlying meanings and connections in the text
- ▶ Composing letters, reports or written arguments
- ▶ Taking part in discussions or debates.

Like any form of exercise these activities will be most successful when you integrate them into your normal life. If you can perform the exercises in a way that becomes a habitual part of your day your raw verbal ability will grow steadily. It is much better to introduce small changes, such as taking the time to complete a daily crossword, than attempt infrequent or overly demanding verbal exercises.

Remember that there is an upper limit to your verbal ability. Just as we can't all grow our muscles to the same size as Mr or Mrs Universe, we can't all grow our verbal ability to the level of Albert Einstein.

What you can do is combine knowledge of the test, your test-taking strategies and practice to develop your verbal ability to its maximum – this will help you achieve your personal best score.

CHAPTER 3
VERBAL COMPREHENSION

Verbal comprehension tests are the simplest form of verbal ability test. These tests are based on clear and straightforward verbal information and a series of true/false questions.

The questions are designed to assess your understanding of the verbal information. You are not required to make decisions or solve complex problems during the test. Your job is to demonstrate that you can read and understand the level of written information that you would encounter in the job itself.

GETTING THE MOST FROM THESE PRACTICE QUESTIONS

These verbal comprehension practice questions are grouped together into three short practice tests. Each practice test mirrors the approach of a real test: there is a short extract of verbal information followed by a series of five questions for you to answer about the information you have read.

You are encouraged to complete each practice test one at a time and to spend time at the end of each short test to review your responses against the correct answers. Once you are happy with your work you can move on to the next test.

The test instructions for these practice tests follow the same format and approach of instructions in real tests – so make sure that you familiarise yourself with these so that you are more prepared when taking an actual test.

Completing the practice tests

Ideally you should complete the practice tests in conditions that are as close to the real testing environment and experience as possible.

▸ Find a quiet place that is free from any distractions.
▸ Read the practice test instructions before beginning the first practice test.
▸ Real tests have strict time limits. Simulate this by giving yourself five minutes per practice test. Start timing from the point you begin reading the verbal information for the test.
▸ Mark your answers in the spaces provided beneath each practice question by fully colouring in the circle for the answer you think is correct.
▸ Do not turn over to the correct answers until you have completed all the practice questions.

Advice for verbal comprehension tests

Remember that while verbal comprehension tests are the simplest type of verbal ability tests, you should not assume that they are straightforward. You need to approach these tests as carefully as you would any other since they can place significant demands on your powers of attention to detail, and ability to correctly interpret verbally presented information.

Verbal comprehension tests require you to employ the fundamental elements of verbal ability: the capability to accurately decipher the true meaning from a passage of verbal information and interpret it correctly. These skills are critical to most jobs, not just those with minimal requirements for verbal ability.

Do not be tempted to skip these practice tests and jump straight to the more difficult verbal reasoning and critical-reasoning practice tests. Completing these verbal comprehension practice tests will greatly benefit your test-taking strategies and level of practice.

When completing a verbal comprehension test, remember these points.

▶ **Read the verbal information carefully before beginning the practice questions.** You do not need to memorise it but you will perform better if you are familiar with the information when attempting the questions.
▶ **Do not simply guess your answers.** You may think that you have a 50:50 chance of getting a true or false question correct by guessing, but there is often a scoring mechanism designed to detect or penalise attempts to guess. Always carefully consider your answers by searching the verbal information for points that either confirm or disconfirm your thoughts about the answer.
▶ **Never base your answers on assumptions.** Look for information that definitely tells you that a given statement is true or false.
▶ **Remember to base your answers on the information given.** Ignore anything you understand to be true or false in the real world.
▶ **Never simply write down your answer without checking it first.** When you think you know the answer

to a question straightaway you should always check your understanding by rereading the pertinent part of the verbal information to make sure you are not mistaken.

▶ **Use any time remaining to check your answers.** If you complete all five questions in a practice test within the five minutes time-limit you should recheck your answers, as you would in a real test. This is good test-taking strategy and you should aim to make it a habit.

Before you begin the practice tests

Read the test instructions carefully before you begin. These instructions have been adapted from real test instructions. When you take a real test you will be presented with instructions that follow this format – so take time to benefit from great familiarity with the language and information they include.

Reviewing your answers

Once you have completed a practice test you can turn over the page to check your responses against the correct answers. Along with each correct answer we have provided some additional help and explanation about the answer. We have also highlighted the text within the verbal information that relates to the correct answer.

These practice tests are too short to make an accurate measurement of your verbal reasoning ability (that's what real tests are for), but we can provide some guidance on what your results mean.

Score of 5	Score of 4	Score of 3	Score of 2	Score of 1
Great performance	Good performance	Average performance	Below average performance	Poor performance

You can review your pattern of incorrect answers to see if you have a tendency to overuse the true or false option when unsure of the correct response. Understanding that you have a tendency in either direction should prompt you to be extra careful when considering your answers to questions that you find more difficult. For these questions you should pay close attention to what the verbal information on which you must base your answers really says.

Once you have reviewed your answers take a short break before attempting the next test.

VERBAL COMPREHENSION PRACTICE TESTS

PRACTICE TEST INSTRUCTIONS

These practice tests each consist of five questions
that relate to verbal information given on the first page of each
test. You are required to use this verbal information to decide
whether each of the statements is **True** or **False**. In order to decide
whether each statement is true or false **use only the given verbal
information contained in the extract**.

You should mark your answers in the answers section below the
questions by filling in the appropriate circle:

(T) TRUE	(F) FALSE
Fill in the circle containing a **T** if you think the statement is **True** from the information given in the extract.	Fill in the circle containing an **F** if you think the statement is **False** from the information given in the extract.

These rules are repeated above the statements. In order to arrive
at your answers use only the verbal information given on the facing
page of each test. **Assume that this given information is correct,
even if it contradicts what you believe to be the case in reality.**

▸ Allow yourself a five-minute time-limit for each of the
practice tests.
▸ You should work quickly and accurately.
▸ If you are not sure of an answer, fill in what you think the
right answer is, but do not simply guess your answers.
▸ Check your answers against the correct answers given on
the pages that follow each practice test.

Remember these important points:

▶ Complete each practice test in a quiet place that is free from any distractions.

▶ Start timing the practice test from the point you begin reading the verbal information.

▶ Mark your answers in the spaces provided beneath each practice question by fully colouring in the circle for the answer you think is correct.

▶ Do not turn over to the correct answers until you have completed all the practice questions.

Please turn over to the first practice test, start timing yourself and read through the verbal information now. You should then start answering the questions as soon as you are ready.

EYE PROTECTION RULES

Eye protection must be worn in certain designated areas. There are also certain jobs for which the law states that you must wear eye protection at all times; some of these jobs are performed outside of the designated areas. You must therefore wear eye protection if you are working in one of the designated areas or if you are working on a job which specifically requires eye protection.

There are different types of eye protection: goggles, face screens and safety spectacles. Simply wearing your own personal spectacles by themselves is not sufficient and could be dangerous.

Even seemingly minor eye injuries have led to blindness so it is vital that you know what to do if you get something in your eye. If you get dust, or other particles, in your eye, immediately inform your supervisor and then go to the First Aid Post – do not let your colleagues try to remove the speck. They may be trying to help but they could make the injury worse.

If you get a chemical in your eye, use the special eye wash equipment provided to sluice the eyeball with cold water. Then report the accident and get medical assistance as soon as possible. You must act quickly with an eye injury – do not just assume it will get better on its own.

TRUE	FALSE
Fill in the circle containing a **T** if you think the statement is **True** from the information given in the extract.	Fill in the circle containing an **F** if you think the statement is **False** from the information given in the extract.

1 Some eye injuries have resulted in blindness.

(T)	(F)
TRUE	FALSE

2 If a chemical gets in your eye, the first thing you should do is to report the accident.

(T)	(F)
TRUE	FALSE

3 Face screens are one type of eye protection.

(T)	(F)
TRUE	FALSE

4 It is a legal requirement to wear eye protection for certain jobs.

(T)	(F)
TRUE	FALSE

5 Personal spectacles provide adequate protection against eye injuries.

(T)	(F)
TRUE	FALSE

EYE PROTECTION RULES

Eye protection must be worn in certain designated areas. There are also **4** **certain jobs for which the law states that you must wear eye protection** at all times; some of these jobs are performed outside of the designated areas. You must therefore wear eye protection if you are working in one of the designated areas or if you are working on a job which specifically requires eye protection.

There are **3** **different types of eye protection: goggles, face screens and safety spectacles.** Simply wearing your own **5** **personal spectacles by themselves is not sufficient and could be dangerous**.

1 **Even seemingly minor eye injuries have led to blindness** so it is vital that you know what to do if you get something in your eye. If you get dust, or other particles, in your eye, immediately inform your supervisor and then go to the First Aid Post – do not let your colleagues try to remove the speck. They may be trying to help but they could make the injury worse.

If you get a chemical in your eye, **2** **use the special eye wash equipment provided to sluice the eyeball with cold water. Then report the accident** and get medical assistance as soon as possible. You must act quickly with an eye injury – do not just assume it will get better on its own.

1   **Some eye injuries have resulted in blindness.**

Correct answer is T: True – you can see that the statement is true in the highlighted text in the third paragraph of the verbal information, which states that even seemingly minor eye injuries have led to blindness.

2   **If a chemical gets in your eye, the first thing you should do is to report the accident.**

Correct answer is F: False – you can see that the statement is false in the highlighted text in the final paragraph, which tells you that you must wash your eye before reporting the accident. This is a good example of a question that tempts you to base your answer on your own beliefs or understanding rather than what the verbal information actually says.

3   **Face screens are one type of eye protection.**

Correct answer is T: True – you can see that the statement is true in the highlighted text in the second paragraph of the verbal information, which lists a number of different types of eye protection, including face screens.

4   **It is a legal requirement to wear eye protection for certain jobs.**

Correct answer is T: True – you can see that the statement is true in the highlighted text in the first paragraph of the verbal information, which says that for certain jobs the law states that you must wear eye protection.

5   **Personal spectacles provide adequate protection against eye injuries.**

Correct answer is F: False – you can see that the statement is false in the highlighted text at the end of the second paragraph, which tells you that spectacles are not sufficient on their own to protect your eyes. This is another example of a question that tempts you to base your answer on your own beliefs or understanding rather than what the verbal information actually says.

How did you do?

Score of 5	Score of 4	Score of 3	Score of 2	Score of 1
Great performance	Good performance	Average performance	Below average performance	Poor performance

HOLIDAY AND SICK LEAVE ENTITLEMENT FOR EMPLOYEES OF NEW WORLD POWER

All staff with less than five years' service are entitled to 20 days' paid holiday per year. A holiday year runs from 1 January to 31 December. Five of these days must be taken during factory closure in the summer. These dates will be advised to members of staff by the end of April in the relevant year. The remaining days may be taken at any time, having obtained line manager's agreement at least one month in advance. Staff with more than five years' service are entitled to 25 days' paid holiday, five of which must be taken during summer closure as above. The remaining days may be taken at any time with line manager's agreement at least one month in advance, as above.

All staff may take up to three days' consecutive sick leave, after which a doctor's certificate must be produced. Staff taking more than 10 days' sick leave in any one year may be required to attend a meeting with the HR manager at the year's end.

Bank holidays are taken on the days specified by law, and are additional to the normal holiday entitlement. Staff who are required to work bank holidays for any reason will be entitled to one day off in lieu which can be taken at any time agreed with the line manager at least two weeks in advance.

TRUE	FALSE
Fill in the circle containing a **T** if you think the statement is **True** from the information given in the extract.	Fill in the circle containing an **F** if you think the statement is **False** from the information given in the extract.

1 All holidays must be agreed by the line manager by the end of April.

(T)	(F)
TRUE	FALSE

2 Staff will be informed of the dates of the factory closure.

(T)	(F)
TRUE	FALSE

3 Employees working on a bank holiday are entitled to a day off in lieu.

(T)	(F)	(C)
TRUE	FALSE	CANNOT SAY

4 Staff have to take at least five of their holiday days in the summer.

(T)	(F)
TRUE	FALSE

5 A doctor's certificate is not needed unless more than 10 consecutive days' sick leave are taken.

(T)	(F)
TRUE	FALSE

HOLIDAY AND SICK LEAVE ENTITLEMENT FOR EMPLOYEES OF NEW WORLD POWER

All staff with less than five years' service are entitled to 20 days' paid holiday per year. A holiday year runs from 1 January to 31 December. **4** **Five of these days must be taken during factory closure in the summer.** These dates will be **2** **advised to members of staff by the end of April** in the relevant year. The remaining days may be taken at any time, **1** **having obtained line manager's agreement at least one month in advance**. Staff with more than five years' service are entitled to 25 days' paid holiday, five of which must be taken during summer closure as above. The remaining days may be taken at any time with line manager's agreement at least one month in advance, as above.

All staff may take **5** **up to three days' consecutive sick leave, after which a doctor's certificate must be produced.** Staff taking more than 10 days' sick leave in any one year may be required to attend a meeting with the HR manager at the year's end.

Bank holidays are taken on the days specified by law, and are additional to the normal holiday entitlement. **3** **Staff who are required to work bank holidays for any reason will be entitled to one day off in lieu** which can be taken at any time agreed with the line manager at least two weeks in advance.

1   **All holidays must be agreed by the line manager by the end of April.**

Correct answer is F: False – you can see that the statement is false in the highlighted text in the first paragraph, which tells you that holiday must be agreed with the manager at least one month in advance. This is a good example of a question that tests your verbal comprehension through the inclusion of similar information elsewhere in the extract – in this case that holiday is advised to staff by the end of April. This illustrates the importance of carefully checking your understanding before answering – and reading the whole of the extract.

2   **Staff will be informed of the dates of the factory closure.**

Correct answer is T: True – you can see that the statement is true in the highlighted text in the first paragraph of the verbal information, which states that holiday is advised to staff by the end of April.

3   **Employees working on a bank holiday are entitled to a day off in lieu.**

Correct answer is T: True – you can see that the statement is true in the highlighted text in the final paragraph of the verbal information, which confirms that the bank holiday entitlement for people who work is a day off in lieu.

4   **Staff have to take at least five of their holiday days in the summer.**

Correct answer is T: True – you can see that the statement is true in the highlighted text in the first paragraph of the verbal information, which states that five days' holiday in summer is compulsory.

5   **A doctor's certificate is not needed unless more than 10 consecutive days' sick leave are taken.**

Correct answer is F: False – you can see that the statement is false in the highlighted text in the second paragraph, which tells you that a doctor's certificate must be produced after three days' sick leave. This is another example of a question that tests your verbal comprehension through the inclusion of similar information elsewhere in the extract – this time the 10 days limit, which relates to the requirement to attend a meeting with HR.

How did you do?

Score of 5	Score of 4	Score of 3	Score of 2	Score of 1
Great performance	Good performance	Average performance	Below average performance	Poor performance

HOLIDAY AND SICK LEAVE ENTITLEMENT FOR EMPLOYEES OF NEW WORLD POWER

All staff with less than five years' service are entitled to 20 days' paid holiday per year. A holiday year runs from 1 January to 31 December. Five of these days must be taken during factory closure in the summer. These dates will be advised to members of staff by the end of April in the relevant year. The remaining days may be taken at any time, having obtained the line manager's agreement at least one month in advance. Staff with more than five years' service are entitled to 25 days' paid holiday, five of which must be taken during summer closure as above. The remaining days may be taken at any time with line manager's agreement at least one month in advance, as above.

All staff may take up to three days' consecutive sick leave, after which a doctor's certificate must be produced. Staff taking more than 10 days' sick leave in any one year may be required to attend a meeting with the HR manager at the year's end.

Bank holidays are taken on the days specified by law, and are additional to the normal holiday entitlement. Staff who are required to work bank holidays for any reason will be entitled to one day off in lieu which can be taken at any time agreed with the line manager at least two weeks in advance.

TRUE	**FALSE**
Fill in the circle containing a **T** if you think the statement is **True** from the information given in the extract.	Fill in the circle containing an **F** if you think the statement is **False** from the information given in the extract.

1   Days off in lieu of bank holidays must be agreed at least one month in advance.

Ⓣ	Ⓕ
TRUE	FALSE

2   Staff receive no pay for holiday taken during factory closure in the summer.

Ⓣ	Ⓕ
TRUE	FALSE

3   Staff with less than five years' service are entitled to 20 days' holiday plus bank holidays.

Ⓣ	Ⓕ	Ⓒ
TRUE	FALSE	CANNOT SAY

4   Staff who have worked for the company for more than five years are entitled to five extra days' leave.

Ⓣ	Ⓕ
TRUE	FALSE

5   The holiday year begins at the end of April.

Ⓣ	Ⓕ
TRUE	FALSE

HOLIDAY AND SICK LEAVE ENTITLEMENT FOR EMPLOYEES OF NEW WORLD POWER

3 **All staff with less than five years' service are entitled to** **2** **20 days' paid holiday** per year. **5** **A holiday year runs from 1 January to 31 December.** **2** **Five of these days must be taken during factory closure in the summer.** These dates will be advised to members of staff by the end of April in the relevant year. The remaining days may be taken at any time, having obtained line manager's agreement at least one month in advance. **4** **Staff with more than five years' service are entitled to 25 days' paid holiday**, five of which must be taken during summer closure as above. The remaining days may be taken at any time with the line manager's agreement at least one month in advance, as above.

All staff may take up to three days' consecutive sick leave, after which a doctor's certificate must be produced. Staff taking more than 10 days' sick leave in any one year may be required to attend a meeting with the HR Manager at the year's end.

3 **Bank holidays** are taken on the days specified by law, and **are additional to the normal holiday entitlement**. Staff who are required to work bank holidays for any reason will be entitled to one day off in lieu which can be taken at any time **1** **agreed with the line manager at least two weeks in advance**.

| **1** | Days off in lieu of bank holidays must be agreed at least one month in advance. |

Correct answer is F: False – you can see that the statement is false in the highlighted text in the final paragraph, which tells you that time off in lieu must be agreed at least two weeks in advance. This is an example of a question that tests your verbal comprehension through the inclusion of similar information elsewhere in the extract – in this case the one month advance period for agreeing holiday (in paragraph one). Your verbal comprehension is also stretched because this question is similar to a previous one, question 1 in Practice test 2. You must take care not to become confused by similar but unrelated details within the verbal information.

| **2** | Staff receive no pay for holiday taken during factory closure in the summer. |

Correct answer is F: False – you can see that the statement is false in two pieces of highlighted text in the first paragraph: the first tells you that employees receive 20 days' paid holiday, and the second tells you that five of these 20 (paid) days are taken during the summer factory closure. This is a more advanced comprehension question because it requires you to link separate details and infer the correct answer. This illustrates the importance of reading the whole extract carefully to understand how the entirety of the information adds up to form the whole picture.

| **3** | Staff with less than five years' service are entitled to 20 days' holiday plus bank holidays. |

Correct answer is T: True – you can see that the statement is true from two pieces of highlighted text. The first is in the first paragraph, which tells you that staff with less than five years' service have a 20-day holiday entitlement. The second is in the final paragraph, which tells you that bank holidays are in addition to this basic holiday entitlement. This is another example of a more advanced comprehension question that requires you to link separate details and infer the correct answer.

| **4** | Staff who have worked for the company for more than five years are entitled to five extra days' leave. |

Correct answer is T: True – you can see that the statement is true in the highlighted text in the first paragraph, which tells you that staff with more than five years' service have a 25-day holiday entitlement, which is five days more than the basic entitlement of 20 days.

| **5** | The holiday year begins at the end of April. |

Correct answer is F: False – you can see that the statement is false in the piece of highlighted text in the first paragraph that tells you that the holiday year runs from 1 January to 31 December. Do not confuse this with the confirmation of holiday leave that happens at the end of April and is mentioned in the same paragraph.

How did you do?

Score of 5	Score of 4	Score of 3	Score of 2	Score of 1
Great performance	Good performance	Average performance	Below average performance	Poor performance

CHAPTER 4
VERBAL REASONING

Verbal reasoning tests are the most widely used form of verbal ability test because they reflect the level of demands in the majority of jobs. The written information in these tests is likely to be more complex than the content of a verbal comprehension test. The multiple-choice format will include a cannot say option.

GETTING THE MOST FROM THESE PRACTICE QUESTIONS

These verbal reasoning practice questions are grouped together into 10 short practice tests. Each practice test mirrors the approach of a real test: there is a short extract of verbal information followed by a series of five questions for you to answer about the information you have read.

The test instructions for these practice tests follow the same format and approach of instructions in real tests – so make sure that you familiarise yourself with these so that you are more prepared when taking an actual test.

You're encouraged to complete each practice test one at a time and to spend time at the end of each short test to review your responses against the correct answers. Once you are happy with your work you can move on to the next test.

Completing the practice tests

Ideally you should complete the practice tests in conditions that are as close to the real testing environment and experience as possible.

▶ Find a quiet place that is free from any distractions.

▶ Read the practice test instructions before beginning the first practice test.

▶ Real tests have strict time limits. Simulate this by giving yourself five minutes per practice test. Start timing from the point you begin reading the verbal information for the test.

▶ Mark your answers in the spaces provided beneath each practice question by fully colouring in the circle for the answer you think is correct.

▶ Do not turn over to the correct answers until you have completed all the practice questions.

Advice for verbal reasoning tests

Remember that verbal reasoning tests are the most commonly used type of verbal test. You are therefore most likely to encounter this level of test than any other. When completing a verbal reasoning test, remember these points to perform at your personal best:

▶ **Read the verbal information carefully before beginning the practice questions.** You do not need to memorise it but you will perform better if you are familiar with the information when attempting the questions.

▶ **Remember to base your answers on the information given.** Ignore anything you understand to be true or false in the real world.

▶ **Never simply write down your answer without checking it first.** When you think you know the answer to a question straightaway you should always check your understanding by rereading the pertinent part of the verbal information to make sure you are not mistaken.

▶ **Use any time remaining to check your answers.** If you complete all five questions in a practice test within the five minutes time-limit you should recheck your answers, as you would in a real test. This is good test-taking strategy and you should aim to make it a habit.

If you have jumped straight to these practice tests without completing the lower level verbal comprehension tests we encourage you to stop and go back. Completing the verbal comprehension practice tests will greatly benefit your test-taking strategies and level of practice.

Before you begin the practice tests

Read the test instructions carefully before you begin.
These instructions have been adapted from real test instructions. When you take a real test you will be presented with instructions that follow this format – so take time to benefit from great familiarity with the language and information they include.

Reviewing your answers

Once you have completed a practice test you can turn over the page to check your responses against the correct answers. Along with each correct answer we have provided some additional help and explanation about the answer. We have also highlighted the text within the verbal information that relates to the correct answer.

These practice tests are too short to make an accurate measurement of your verbal reasoning ability (that's what real tests are for), but we can provide some guidance about what your results mean:

Score of 5	Score of 4	Score of 3	Score of 2	Score of 1
Great performance	Good performance	Average performance	Below average performance	Poor performance

If you have scored less than your ideal personal best score then you should look at the pattern of your responses – do you tend to answer specific types of question incorrectly? With verbal reasoning tests it is often the 'cannot say' questions that cause people the most trouble. Below is some advice for improving your performance against each of the response types.

Is the correct answer true?	Before answering 'true' check your answer by identifying the text in the verbal information that confirms that the statement is true.
Is the correct answer false?	Before answering 'false' check your answer by identifying the text in the verbal information that confirms that the statement is false.
Is the correct answer cannot say?	If you cannot find any text in the verbal information that definitively tells you the statement is true or false then you cannot say.

You can also use this as a process for answering questions that you find difficult when you are taking a real test by working through each of the three points to identify the correct answer.

Once you have reviewed your answers take a short break before attempting the next test.

VERBAL
REASONING
PRACTICE TESTS

PRACTICE TEST INSTRUCTIONS

These practice tests each consist of five questions that relate to verbal information given on the first page of each test. You are required to use this verbal information to evaluate the statements that are presented next to the text. You should mark your answers in the spaces provided below each of the questions by filling in the appropriate circle, A, B, or C according to these rules:

Ⓐ TRUE	Ⓑ FALSE	Ⓒ CANNOT SAY
Fill in **A** if the statement is **True** from the information given.	Fill in **B** if the statement is **False** from the information given.	Fill in **C** if you **Cannot say** for certain from the information given whether the statement is true or false.

These rules are repeated above the statements. In order to arrive at your answers use only the verbal information given on the facing page of each test. **Assume that this given information is correct, even if it contradicts what you believe to be the case in reality.**

- ▸ Allow yourself a five-minute time-limit for each of the practice tests.
- ▸ You should work quickly and accurately.
- ▸ If you are not sure of an answer, fill in what you think the right answer is, but do not simply guess your answers.
- ▸ Check your answers against the correct answers given on the pages that follow each practice test.

Remember these important points:

▶ Complete each practice test in a quiet place that is free from any distractions.

▶ Start timing the practice test from the point you begin reading the verbal information.

▶ Mark your answers in the spaces provided beneath each practice question by fully colouring in the circle for the answer you think is correct.

▶ Do not turn over to the correct answers until you have completed all the practice questions.

Please turn over to the first practice test, start timing yourself and read through the verbal information now. You should then start answering the questions as soon as you are ready.

CHAMPIONSHIP RECORDS: PROPOSAL FOR BANK LOAN

Prepared by: Rob Gordon, Manager, Championship Records
For: Mr P. F. James, The Manager, The Southern Bank plc

Nature of business

Rob Gordon is the sole owner of Championship Records, a retail outlet currently selling compact discs (CDs), records and other media to the general public. The business has one store in a favourable location in the High Street. Championship Records was founded by Rob Gordon and began trading four years ago. Since the first year of trading, the store has doubled its turnover and, last year, made a profit of 40% of turnover. The store has a loyal customer base, and currently advertises by word of mouth and small adverts in the local paper.

Reasons for requiring bank loan

1. To finance the refurbishment of the store

The store has not been decorated since the business began trading. A total refurbishment programme is therefore proposed which will include a bright colour scheme (inside and out), chrome-edged storage units, the installation of five auditory booths (complete with an automatic counter-to-booth CD selection system), and new carpets. Rob Gordon has already obtained rough estimates from three design consultancy firms as to the likely costs of such a refurbishment. Once the bank loan has been secured, one of these three design firms will be appointed.

2. To finance new marketing campaigns

As well as redesigning the store's interior/exterior, the design consultancy will provide advice about new advertising campaigns and promotional activities. In keeping with the business's more upmarket image, it is proposed that the name be changed from 'Championship Records' to 'Jumpin' Records' once the refurbishment programme is complete. The marketing campaigns are expected to focus on local and regional newspapers, posters and radio coverage. Various promotions will also take place on a regular basis within the store (special offers, bi-monthly sales, competitions etc).

Expected financial benefits

Once the bank loan has been paid off, it is expected that the financial benefits from this investment will be visible in the form of increased profits. It is anticipated that two years after the investment has been made, the profits will double.

A	B	C
TRUE	**FALSE**	**CANNOT SAY**
Fill in **A** if the statement is **True** from the information given.	Fill in **B** if the statement is **False** from the information given.	Fill in **C** if you **Cannot say** for certain from the information given whether the statement is true or false.

1 The business is currently known as 'Jumpin' Records'.

(A)	(B)	(C)
TRUE	FALSE	CANNOT SAY

2 Word of mouth is a better form of advertising than the local paper.

(A)	(B)	(C)
TRUE	FALSE	CANNOT SAY

3 **Championship Records'** profits have increased every year since the store opened.

(A)	(B)	(C)
TRUE	FALSE	CANNOT SAY

4 **Championship Records** will employ a design consultancy to take care of the refurbishment of the store.

(A)	(B)	(C)
TRUE	FALSE	CANNOT SAY

5 Financial benefits from the refurbishment and new marketing will not be visible until after the bank loan has been paid off.

(A)	(B)	(C)
TRUE	FALSE	CANNOT SAY

CHAMPIONSHIP RECORDS: PROPOSAL FOR BANK LOAN

Prepared by: Rob Gordon, Manager, Championship Records
For: Mr P. F. James, The Manager, The Southern Bank plc

Nature of business

Rob Gordon is the sole owner of Championship Records, a retail outlet currently selling compact discs (CDs), records and other media to the general public. The business has one store in a favourable location in the High Street. Championship Records was founded by Rob Gordon and began trading four years ago. **3 Since the first year of trading, the store has doubled its turnover and, last year, made a profit of 40% of turnover.** The store has a loyal customer base, **2 and currently advertises by word of mouth and small adverts in the local paper.**

Reasons for requiring bank loan

1. To finance the refurbishment of the store

The store has not been decorated since the business began trading. A total refurbishment programme is therefore proposed which will include a bright colour scheme (inside and out), chrome-edged storage units, the installation of five auditory booths (complete with an automatic counter-to-booth CD selection system), and new carpets. Rob Gordon has already **4 obtained rough estimates from three design consultancy firms** as to the likely costs of such a refurbishment. Once the bank loan has been secured, **4 one of these three design firms will be appointed.**

2. To finance new marketing campaigns

As well as redesigning the store's interior/exterior, the design consultancy will provide advice about new advertising campaigns and promotional activities. In keeping with the business's more up-market image, it is proposed that the **1 name be changed from 'Championship Records' to 'Jumpin' Records' once the refurbishment programme is complete.** The marketing campaigns are expected to focus on local and regional newspapers, posters and radio coverage. Various promotions will also take place on a regular basis within the store (special offers, bi-monthly sales, competitions etc).

Expected financial benefits

5 Once the bank loan has been paid off, it is expected that the financial benefits from this investment will be visible in the form of increased profits. It is anticipated that two years after the investment has been made, the profits will double.

| **1** | The business is currently known as 'Jumpin' Records'. |

Correct answer is B: False – you can see that the statement is false in the highlighted text in the paragraph about marketing campaigns in the verbal information – Championship Records will be renamed Jumpin' Records once the refurbishment is complete. The correct answer is therefore False.

| **2** | Word-of-mouth is a better form of advertising than the local paper. |

Correct answer is C: Cannot say – you can see from the highlighted text in the second paragraph that Championship Records uses both the local paper and word-of-mouth for advertising; no information is given about whether one form of advertising is better than the other. This is a good example of a cannot say question; the verbal information is ambiguous – it does not say for certain whether one form of advertising is better than the other. We must not make the mistake of basing our answer on what we think is true in the real world. We cannot say whether the statement is true or false – it might be either, so the correct answer is therefore Cannot say.

| **3** . | Championship Records' profits have increased every year since the store opened. |

Correct answer is C: Cannot say – you can see from the highlighted text in the second paragraph that Championship Records made a profit of 40% last year. But we cannot be certain whether this performance happened every year – for instance, profits may have dipped in years 1–3 of trading. We do not have enough information to say that this statement is true or false, so the correct answer is Cannot say.

| **4** | Championship Records will employ a design consultancy to take care of the refurbishment of the store. |

Correct answer is A: True – you can see that the statement is true in the highlighted text in the fourth paragraph of the verbal information – a design consultancy will be appointed to implement the refurbishment.

| **5** | Financial benefits from the refurbishment and new marketing will not be visible until after the bank loan has been paid off. |

Correct answer is A: True – you can see that the statement is true in the highlighted text in the final paragraph of the verbal information – increased profits will be visible once the bank loan is paid off.

How did you do?

Score of 5	Score of 4	Score of 3	Score of 2	Score of 1
Great performance	Good performance	Average performance	Below average performance	Poor performance

Murray Peterson
Asterisk Design Consultancy
Kerning Road
Brighton
BN1 4AP

Dear Mr Peterson

Re: Store refurbishment designs

Many thanks for your proposal to refurbish Championship Records. I have looked at it over the last few days and overall I am very impressed.

I particularly liked the raised till area which you proposed, although I think that it might cause us some security problems. Last year we cut our losses due to theft by 30% and I want to ensure that they do not increase again this year. Can you make any recommendations to increase security? Anodyne Designs, who refurbished our main competitor, Suicide Notes, included an electronic security system in their proposal. Although it was expensive they can show that it will cut crime and I think that it might be a good investment.

I am rather unhappy with the design for the new neon sign which you proposed for the store front. As you know the store front is 11.4m wide and so I think that a sign which is only 4m across will be lost. I understand that if the sign is wider it will have to be taller to stay in proportion and that it will obstruct the door, but we want the sign to be seen from the bus stop on the other side of the road.

Your proposal did not include designs for new listening posts which I want at the back of the store. I have assumed that the listening posts will follow the same idea as the CD racks you propose, which I like very much.

Even though I like your ideas more than those submitted by your rivals, I am rather concerned by the costs you indicated. Why is everything so expensive? It must be possible to save money without compromising the quality of the design. If you can think of ways to cut the cost by 10% and can answer the issues I raised above then the project is yours.

I must decide on a design within the next few weeks and so would be grateful if you would submit an amended proposal by the end of this week. I look forward to hearing from you.

Yours sincerely

Rob Gordon
Manager, Championship Records

A	B	C
TRUE	**FALSE**	**CANNOT SAY**
Fill in **A** if the statement is **True** from the information given.	Fill in **B** if the statement is **False** from the information given.	Fill in **C** if you **Cannot say** for certain from the information given whether the statement is true or false.

1   Last year losses due to theft increased.

Ⓐ	Ⓑ	Ⓒ
TRUE	FALSE	CANNOT SAY

2   **Suicide Notes** has installed an electronic security system.

Ⓐ	Ⓑ	Ⓒ
TRUE	FALSE	CANNOT SAY

3   **Asterisk Design's** proposal indicates that the neon sign will be the same width as the store front.

Ⓐ	Ⓑ	Ⓒ
TRUE	FALSE	CANNOT SAY

4   Rob has indicated what **Asterisk Design** must do in order to win the business.

Ⓐ	Ⓑ	Ⓒ
TRUE	FALSE	CANNOT SAY

5   Rob was very impressed with Murray Peterson's proposal.

Ⓐ	Ⓑ	Ⓒ
TRUE	FALSE	CANNOT SAY

Murray Peterson
Asterisk Design Consultancy
Kerning Road
Brighton
BN1 4AP

Dear Mr Peterson

Re: Store refurbishment designs

Many thanks for your proposal to refurbish Championship Records. **5 I have looked at it over the last few days and overall I am very impressed.**

I particularly liked the raised till area which you proposed, although I think that it might cause us some security problems. **1 Last year we cut our losses due to theft by 30%** and I want to ensure that they do not increase again this year. Can you make any recommendations to increase security? **2 Anodyne Designs, who refurbished our main competitor, Suicide Notes, included an electronic security system in their proposal.** Although it was expensive they can show that it will cut crime and I think that it might be a good investment.

I am rather unhappy with the design for the new neon sign which you proposed for the store front. **3 As you know the store front is 11.4m wide and so I think that a sign which is only 4m across** will be lost. I understand that if the sign is wider it will have to be taller to stay in proportion and that it will obstruct the door, but we want the sign to be seen from the bus stop on the other side of the road.

Your proposal did not include designs for new listening posts which I want at the back of the store. I have assumed that the listening posts will follow the same idea as the CD racks you propose which I like very much.

Even though I like your ideas more than those submitted by your rivals, I am rather concerned by the costs you indicated. Why is everything so expensive? It must be possible to save money without compromising the quality of the design. **4 If you can think of ways to cut the cost by 10% and can answer the issues I raised above then the project is yours.**

I must decide on a design within the next few weeks and so would be grateful if you would submit an amended proposal by the end of this week. I look forward to hearing from you.

Yours sincerely

Rob Gordon
Manager, Championship Records

1	Last year losses due to theft increased.

Correct answer is B: False – you can see that the statement is false in the highlighted text in the second paragraph – Championship Records reduced losses from theft by 30% last year. The correct answer is therefore False.

2	Suicide Notes has installed an electronic security system.

Correct answer is C: Cannot say – you can see from the highlighted text in the second paragraph that the design consultancy, Anodyne, who refurbished Suicide Notes, included an electronic security system in their proposal. No information is given stating whether Suicide Notes has such a system installed. It would be wrong to infer that just because Anodyne Designs proposed a system for Championship Records that they installed one for Suicide Notes. We cannot say whether the statement is true or false – it might be either, so the correct answer is Cannot say.

3	Asterisk Design's proposal indicates that the neon sign will be the same width as the store front.

Correct answer is B: False – you can see that the statement is false in the highlighted text in the third paragraph – the proposed neon sign is 4m across while the store front is over 11m across.

4	Rob has indicated what Asterisk Design must do in order to win the business.

Correct answer is A: True – you can see that the statement is true in the highlighted text in the fifth paragraph of the verbal information – Rob will award the business to Asterisk Designs if they can reduce the costs by 10% and provide answers to the issues raised.

5	Rob was very impressed with Murray Peterson's proposal.

Correct answer is A: True – you can see that the statement is true in the highlighted text in the first paragraph of the verbal information – Rob says he is very impressed.

How did you do?

Score of 5	Score of 4	Score of 3	Score of 2	Score of 1
Great performance	Good performance	Average performance	Below average performance	Poor performance

Murray Peterson
Asterisk Design Consultancy
Kerning Road
Brighton
BN1 4AP

Dear Mr Peterson

Re: Store refurbishment designs

Many thanks for your proposal to refurbish Championship Records. I have looked at it over the last few days and overall I am very impressed.

I particularly liked the raised till area which you proposed, although I think that it might cause us some security problems. Last year we cut our losses due to theft by 30% and I want to ensure that they do not increase again this year. Can you make any recommendations to increase security? Anodyne Designs, who refurbished our main competitor, Suicide Notes, included an electronic security system in their proposal. Although it was expensive they can show that it will cut crime and I think that it might be a good investment.

I am rather unhappy with the design for the new neon sign which you proposed for the store front. As you know the store front is 11.4m wide and so I think that a sign which is only 4m across will be lost. I understand that if the sign is wider it will have to be taller to stay in proportion and that it will obstruct the door, but we want the sign to be seen from the bus stop on the other side of the road.

Your proposal did not include designs for new listening posts which I want at the back of the store. I have assumed that the listening posts will follow the same idea as the CD racks you propose, which I like very much.

Even though I like your ideas more than those submitted by your rivals, I am rather concerned by the costs you indicated. Why is everything so expensive? It must be possible to save money without compromising the quality of the design. If you can think of ways to cut the cost by 10% and can answer the issues I raised above then the project is yours.

I must decide on a design within the next few weeks and so would be grateful if you would submit an amended proposal by the end of this week. I look forward to hearing from you.

Yours sincerely

Rob Gordon
Manager, Championship Records

A	B	C
TRUE	**FALSE**	**CANNOT SAY**
Fill in **A** if the statement is **True** from the information given.	Fill in **B** if the statement is **False** from the information given.	Fill in **C** if you **Cannot say** for certain from the information given whether the statement is true or false.

1   Rob is not deterred by the likely cost of an electronic security system.

Ⓐ	Ⓑ	Ⓒ
TRUE	FALSE	CANNOT SAY

2   The proposal from Murray Peterson was incomplete.

Ⓐ	Ⓑ	Ⓒ
TRUE	FALSE	CANNOT SAY

3   **Asterisk Design** submitted the most expensive refurbishment proposal.

Ⓐ	Ⓑ	Ⓒ
TRUE	FALSE	CANNOT SAY

4   Rob prefers the ideas proposed by **Asterisk Design's** rivals.

Ⓐ	Ⓑ	Ⓒ
TRUE	FALSE	CANNOT SAY

5   If **Asterisk Design** lower their price by 10% they will be awarded the business.

Ⓐ	Ⓑ	Ⓒ
TRUE	FALSE	CANNOT SAY

Murray Peterson
Asterisk Design Consultancy
Kerning Road
Brighton
BN1 4AP

Dear Mr Peterson

Re: Store refurbishment designs

Many thanks for your proposal to refurbish Championship Records. I have looked at it over the last few days and overall I am very impressed.

I particularly liked the raised till area which you proposed, although I think that it might cause us some security problems. Last year we cut our losses due to theft by 30% and I want to ensure that they do not increase again this year. Can you make any recommendations to increase security? Anodyne Designs who refurbished our main competitor, Suicide Notes, included an electronic security system in their proposal. **1 Although it was expensive they can show that it will cut crime and I think that it might be a good investment.**

I am rather unhappy with the design for the new neon sign which you proposed for the store front. As you know the store front is 11.4m wide and so I think that a sign which is only 4m across will be lost. I understand that if the sign is wider it will have to be taller to stay in proportion and that it will obstruct the door, but we want the sign to be seen from the bus stop on the other side of the road.

2 Your proposal did not include designs for new listening posts which I want at the back of the store. I have assumed that the listening posts will follow the same idea as the CD racks you propose which I like very much.

Even though **3** **4 I like your ideas more than those submitted by your rivals, I am rather concerned by the costs you indicated. Why is everything so expensive?** It must be possible to save money without compromising the quality of the design. **5 If you can think of ways to cut the cost by 10% and can answer the issues I raised above then the project is yours.**

I must decide on a design within the next few weeks and so would be grateful if you would submit an amended proposal by the end of this week. I look forward to hearing from you.

Yours sincerely

Rob Gordon
Manager, Championship Records

1   Rob is not deterred by the likely cost of an electronic security system.

Correct answer is A: True – you can see that the statement is true in the highlighted text in the second paragraph of the verbal information – Rob states that the system was expensive but thinks it might be a good investment because of its effects on crime rates in the store.

2   The proposal from Murray Peterson was incomplete.

Correct answer is A: True – you can see that the statement is true in the highlighted text in the fourth paragraph of the verbal information – the proposal does not include designs for listening posts.

3   **Asterisk Design** submitted the most expensive refurbishment proposal.

Correct answer is C: Cannot say – you can see from the highlighted text in the fifth paragraph that Rob describes the costs as expensive but does not state whether they were more or less than those in the rival proposals. We cannot say whether the statement is true or false – it might be either, so the correct answer is Cannot say.

4   Rob prefers the ideas proposed by **Asterisk Design's** rivals.

Correct answer is B: False – you can see that the statement is false in the highlighted text in the fifth paragraph – Rob prefers the ideas from Asterisk Design to those of their rivals.

5   If **Asterisk Design** lower their price by 10% they will be awarded the business.

Correct answer is C: Cannot say – you can see from the highlighted text in the fifth paragraph that Rob invites Asterisk Design to cut their costs by 10% and provide answers to the issues he has raised. It is unclear whether a price reduction is sufficient alone to win the business. We should not make the mistake of being influenced by the correct answer to Practice test 2 (question 4) and mistakenly answer this question as true. Equally we must not be tempted to answer this question as false because Rob describes two factors that Asterisk must address to win their business in unclear. Because the link between the 10% cost reduction and winning the business is unclear we cannot be certain whether the statement is true or false, so the correct answer is Cannot say.

How did you do?

Score of 5	Score of 4	Score of 3	Score of 2	Score of 1
Great performance	Good performance	Average performance	Below average performance	Poor performance

WIREDFORSOUND.COM – THE NEW ONLINE MUSIC STORE

This month sees the launch of a new venture in online music services. **Wiredforsound.com** offers its customers the choice between a range of music downloads, mobile phone ringtones and conventional products like CDs and DVDs.

Unlike existing online music stores, **Wiredforsound.com** will exclusively offer music from unsigned and independent artists as well as established acts whose products are marketed by major record companies. Customers will be able to listen online to selections from unsigned musicians and download tracks free of charge. This reflects the **Wiredforsound.com** mission of supporting talented new acts in the early stages of their careers.

Wiredforsound.com also offers music from established artists, which customers can order online and benefit from big savings on high street prices. Sales of DVDs, CDs and other music products downloads from established artists help subsidise the free downloads of music by unsigned acts.

Rob Gordon launched **Wiredforsound.com** as a reaction to established record companies who in the past have operated a monopoly over music. They decided which music customers should listen to by restricting their marketing activities to safe acts. This has led to a succession of 'production line' popstars with little creativity and nothing new to say.

A	B	C
TRUE	**FALSE**	**CANNOT SAY**
Fill in **A** if the statement is **True** from the information given.	Fill in **B** if the statement is **False** from the information given.	Fill in **C** if you **Cannot say** for certain from the information given whether the statement is true or false.

1 The online music service **Wiredforsound.com** does not sell mobile phone ringtones.

Ⓐ	Ⓑ	Ⓒ
TRUE	FALSE	CANNOT SAY

2 Music downloads from established artists are less popular than downloads from unsigned acts.

Ⓐ	Ⓑ	Ⓒ
TRUE	FALSE	CANNOT SAY

3 It costs nothing to listen to an unsigned artist on **Wiredforsound.com**.

Ⓐ	Ⓑ	Ⓒ
TRUE	FALSE	CANNOT SAY

4 Online prices will be more expensive than high street prices.

Ⓐ	Ⓑ	Ⓒ
TRUE	FALSE	CANNOT SAY

5 Record companies traditionally spend more money on marketing acts that are more certain to be a commercial success.

Ⓐ	Ⓑ	Ⓒ
TRUE	FALSE	CANNOT SAY

WIREDFORSOUND.COM – THE NEW ONLINE MUSIC STORE

This month sees the launch of a new venture in online music services. **Wiredforsound.com** offers its customers the choice between ranges of **1 music downloads, mobile phone ringtones and conventional products like CDs and DVDs.**

Unlike existing online music stores, **Wiredforsound.com** will **2 exclusively offer music from unsigned and independent artists as well as established acts** whose products are marketed by major record companies. **3 Customers will be able to listen online to selections from unsigned musicians and download tracks free of charge.** This reflects the **Wiredforsound.com** mission of supporting talented new acts in the early stages of their careers.

Wiredforsound.com also offers music from established artists, which customers can **4 order online and benefit from big savings on high street prices**. **2 Sales of DVDs, CDs and other music products downloads from established artists help subsidise the free downloads of music by unsigned acts.**

Rob Gordon launched **Wiredforsound.com** as a reaction to established record companies who in the past have operated a monopoly over music. They decided which music customers should listen to by **5 restricting their marketing activities to safe acts.** This has led to a succession of 'production line' popstars with little creativity and nothing new to say.

1	The online music service **Wiredforsound.com** does not sell mobile phone ringtones.

Correct answer is B: False – you can see that the statement is false in the highlighted text in the first paragraph – **Wiredforsound.com** does sell ringtones.

2	Music downloads from established artists are less popular than downloads from unsigned acts.

Correct answer is C: Cannot say – you can see from the information in paragraphs 2 and 3 that **Wireforsound.com** will offer unsigned acts but there is no information about their relative popularity compared to established acts. While we may believe this statement to be true based on our own experiences, we cannot say from the information given whether the statement is true or false, so the correct answer is Cannot say.

3	It costs nothing to listen to an unsigned artist on **Wiredforsound.com**.

Correct answer is A: True – you can see that the statement is true in the highlighted text in the second paragraph of the verbal information – customers can listen online and download unsigned acts for free.

4	Online prices will be more expensive than high street prices.

Correct answer is B: False – you can see that the statement is false in the highlighted text in the third paragraph – online prices offer big savings on high street prices.

5	Record companies traditionally spend more money on marketing acts that are more certain to be a commercial success.

Correct answer is A: True – you can see that the statement is true in the highlighted text in the final paragraph of the verbal information – record companies restrict their marketing activities to safe acts.

How did you do?

Score of 5	Score of 4	Score of 3	Score of 2	Score of 1
Great performance	Good performance	Average performance	Below average performance	Poor performance

WELCOME TO FAIRSHARE

FairShare was founded by Rob Gordon following his success as a music promoter and owner of the online record store Wiredforsound.com. Rob then became determined to help promote smaller, unsigned artists, but soon decided that there were too many different artistic mediums to focus exclusively on bands. It is from this idea that the reality of the all-encompassing sharing network **FairShare** was born.

The **FairShare** website is a place to explore and share creative talent. Music, images and videos created by users can be copied onto a publicly accessible **FairShare** storage computer. From here these files are available for any user to download onto their own computer.

It is this 'uploading' and 'downloading' of files by individuals which enables previously unknown talent to be recognised and freely shared across the globe.

FairShare doesn't cost its users a penny. Funds generated through advertising and the sale of **FairShare** merchandise enable **FairShare** to operate for the good of those who use it to keep sharing alive.

A	B	C
TRUE	**FALSE**	**CANNOT SAY**
Fill in **A** if the statement is **True** from the information given.	Fill in **B** if the statement is **False** from the information given.	Fill in **C** if you **Cannot say** for certain from the information given whether the statement is true or false.

1

'Uploading' files enables users to copy their own music, images and videos onto a publicly accessible storage computer.

(A)	(B)	(C)
TRUE	FALSE	CANNOT SAY

2

Most of the files uploaded onto **FairShare** are videos which users have filmed themselves.

(A)	(B)	(C)
TRUE	FALSE	CANNOT SAY

3

Users pay a monthly fee to share their creative work on **FairShare**.

(A)	(B)	(C)
TRUE	FALSE	CANNOT SAY

4

Income is generated by **FairShare** products.

(A)	(B)	(C)
TRUE	FALSE	CANNOT SAY

5

Rob Gordon is not the sole owner of **FairShare**.

(A)	(B)	(C)
TRUE	FALSE	CANNOT SAY

WELCOME TO FAIRSHARE

5 FairShare was founded by Rob Gordon following his success as a music promoter and owner of the online record store Wiredforsound.com. Rob then became determined to help promote smaller, unsigned artists, but soon decided that there were too many different artistic mediums to focus exclusively on bands. It is from this idea that the reality of the all-encompassing sharing network **FairShare** was born.

The **FairShare** website is a place to explore and share creative talent. **1 2 Music, images and videos created by users can be copied onto a publicly accessible FairShare storage computer**. From here these files are available for any user to download onto their own computer.

1 It is this 'uploading' and 'downloading' of files by individuals which enables previously unknown talent to be recognised and freely shared across the globe.

3 FairShare doesn't cost its users a penny. 4 Funds generated through advertising and the sale of FairShare merchandise enable **FairShare** to operate for the good of those who use it to keep sharing alive.

| **1** | 'Uploading' files enables users to copy their own music, images and videos onto a publicly accessible storage computer. |

Correct answer is A: True – you can see that the statement is true in the highlighted text in the second paragraph of the verbal information – users can copy their files onto the storage computer. This process is called 'uploading' in the third paragraph. This is an example of a verbal reasoning question that requires you to make a logical inference based on two separate pieces of information. Copying files onto the publicly accessible storage computer is later defined as 'uploading', so the statement is true.

| **2** | Most of the files uploaded onto **FairShare** are videos which users have filmed themselves. |

Correct answer is C: Cannot say – you can see from the highlighted text in the second paragraph that users can upload music, images and videos that they have created but no information is given about whether one of these three types of files is uploaded the most. We cannot say whether the statement is true or false – videos may or may not be the most common upload – we should not base our answer on what we think is true in the real world.

| **3** | Users pay a monthly fee to share their creative work on **FairShare**. |

Correct answer is B: False – you can see that the statement is false in the highlighted text in the final paragraph – **FairShare** is free to use.

| **4** | Income is generated by **FairShare** products. |

Correct answer is A: True – you can see that the statement is true in the highlighted text in the second line of the final paragraph of the verbal information – income is generated by advertising and merchandise sales.

| **5** | Rob Gordon is not the sole owner of **FairShare**. |

Correct answer is C: Cannot say – you can see from the highlighted text in the first line that Rob founded **FairShare**. This could lead us to assume that Rob is the sole owner and therefore answer this question as False. However, no specific information is given about the ownership of **FairShare**. We cannot say whether the statement is true or false and should not base our answer on an assumption. Because Rob may or may not be the sole owner, the correct answer is Cannot say.

How did you do?

Score of 5	Score of 4	Score of 3	Score of 2	Score of 1
Great performance	Good performance	Average performance	Below average performance	Poor performance

NEW WORLD POWER CONSERVATION WORK

New World Power (NWP) continues to build on its reputation as Europe's most environmentally friendly energy company with new measures at Diablo's Creek, the site of the NWP nuclear power station near Sheerness.

Diablo's Creek attracts a wide range of wildlife not normally seen in the UK – thanks to the efforts of NWP engineers at the new power station. They have worked with scientists and the environmentalists to create an internationally recognised conservation area for many species of birds.

The power station takes cooling water from the creek and returns it up to 10°C warmer, which has made it an attractive home for some plants and animals normally found in the Mediterranean and other warmer climates. But it is the birds that are the real focus of the conservation work. In total 32 species of birds have been recorded there, in particular migrating birds such as swans and ducks, which use the site as a warm winter refuge.

The project has been running for over five years and the dock is seen as an outstanding example of how industrial needs and conservation interests can work side by side. The success of the project has recently been recognised by the Environment Agency.

A	B	C
TRUE	**FALSE**	**CANNOT SAY**
Fill in **A** if the statement is **True** from the information given.	Fill in **B** if the statement is **False** from the information given.	Fill in **C** if you **Cannot say** for certain from the information given whether the statement is true or false.

1 The Environment Agency considers the Diablo's Creek project a success.

(A)	(B)	(C)
TRUE	FALSE	CANNOT SAY

2 NWP engineers started work on the conservation project over five years ago.

(A)	(B)	(C)
TRUE	FALSE	CANNOT SAY

3 The conservation project has won awards.

(A)	(B)	(C)
TRUE	FALSE	CANNOT SAY

4 The Diablo's Creek nuclear power station is environmentally friendly.

(A)	(B)	(C)
TRUE	FALSE	CANNOT SAY

5 The Diablo's Creek project has received recognition from around the world.

(A)	(B)	(C)
TRUE	FALSE	CANNOT SAY

NEW WORLD POWER CONSERVATION WORK

New World Power (NWP) continues to build on its reputation as Europe's **4** **most environmentally friendly energy company with new measures at Diablo's Creek, the site of the NWP nuclear power station near Sheerness**.

Diablo's Creek attracts a wide range of wildlife not normally seen in the UK – thanks to the efforts of NWP engineers at the new power station. They have worked with scientists and the environmentalists to create an **5** **internationally recognised conservation area** for many species of birds.

The power station takes cooling water from the creek and returns it up to 10°C warmer, which has made it an attractive home for some plants and animals normally found in the Mediterranean and other warmer climates. But it is the birds that are the real focus of the conservation work. In total 32 species of birds have been recorded there, in particular migrating birds such as swans and ducks, which use the site as a warm winter refuge.

2 **The project has been running for over five years** and the dock is seen as an outstanding example of how industrial needs and conservation interests can work side by side. **1** **3** **The success of the project has recently been recognised by the Environment Agency**.

1   The Environment Agency considers the Diablo's Creek project a success.

Correct answer is A: True – you can see that the statement is true in the highlighted text in the final paragraph of the verbal information - the Environment Agency has recognised the success of the project.

2   NWP engineers started work on the conservation project over five years ago.

Correct answer is C: Cannot say – you can see from the highlighted text in the final paragraph of the verbal information that the project has been running for over five years. Work could have begun on the project before this but the text does not say if the work was begun by NWP engineers so the correct answer is Cannot say.

3   The conservation project has won awards.

Correct answer is C: Cannot say – you can see from the highlighted text in the final paragraph of the verbal information that the project has been recognised but we cannot be certain whether or not it has won any awards. The correct answer is therefore Cannot say.

4   The Diablo's Creek nuclear power station is environmentally friendly.

Correct answer is C: Cannot say – you can see from the highlighted text in the first paragraph of the verbal information that NWP has an environmentally friendly reputation and the third paragraph describes measures introduced to produce environmental benefits from the operation of the power station. It would be wrong to infer from these pieces of information alone that this makes the power station environmentally friendly though. It would also be wrong to presume, based on our understanding of real life information, that the statement is false. Because of this uncertainty from the information given the correct answer is Cannot say.

5   The Diablo's Creek project has received recognition from around the world.

Correct answer is A: True – you can see that the statement is true in the highlighted text in the second paragraph of the verbal information – the project has received international recognition.

How did you do?

Score of 5	Score of 4	Score of 3	Score of 2	Score of 1
Great performance	Good performance	Average performance	Below average performance	Poor performance

THE CLIMATE CHANGE CHALLENGE

Climate change is the biggest single environmental issue the world faces right now. The Earth's climate was relatively stable for about 10,000 years, but now the average global temperature is rising. This rise in temperature is causing changing rainfall patterns, a rise in sea levels, glaciers to melt, and extreme weather incidents are becoming more frequent in some parts of the world.

The rise in global temperature is caused by something known as the 'greenhouse effect'. The Earth is surrounded by a warm-air blanket of gases such as carbon dioxide, nitrous oxide and methane, which keep the Earth warm. The problem is that this blanket is getting thicker, trapping in heat like a greenhouse, causing the climate to get warmer.

Research has shown that the modern day lifestyle is contributing to climate change as greenhouse gases are released when we burn fuels such as gas, coal and oil for energy. However, there is plenty that can be done to decrease the volume of greenhouse gases we produce and slow the process of global warming – for example, by using renewable energy resources and making sure that homes and businesses are as energy efficient as possible.

A	B	C
TRUE	**FALSE**	**CANNOT SAY**
Fill in **A** if the statement is **True** from the information given.	Fill in **B** if the statement is **False** from the information given.	Fill in **C** if you **Cannot say** for certain from the information given whether the statement is true or false.

1 Home owners and businesses are already working towards being more energy efficient.

Ⓐ	Ⓑ	Ⓒ
TRUE	FALSE	CANNOT SAY

2 Our lifestyle has no connection with climate change.

Ⓐ	Ⓑ	Ⓒ
TRUE	FALSE	CANNOT SAY

3 The greenhouse effect has global consequences.

Ⓐ	Ⓑ	Ⓒ
TRUE	FALSE	CANNOT SAY

4 In the future the sea level will be higher than it is now.

Ⓐ	Ⓑ	Ⓒ
TRUE	FALSE	CANNOT SAY

5 Climate change is the only environmental issue people need to be concerned about.

Ⓐ	Ⓑ	Ⓒ
TRUE	FALSE	CANNOT SAY

THE CLIMATE CHANGE CHALLENGE

5 Climate change is the biggest single environmental issue the world faces right now. The Earth's climate was relatively stable for about 10,000 years, but now the average global temperature is rising. This rise in temperature is **4** causing changing rainfall patterns, a rise in sea levels, glaciers to melt, and extreme weather incidents are becoming more frequent in some parts of the world.

3 The rise in global temperature is caused by something known as the 'greenhouse effect'. The Earth is surrounded by a warm-air blanket of gases such as carbon dioxide, nitrous oxide and methane, which keep the Earth warm. The problem is that this blanket is getting thicker, trapping in heat like a greenhouse, causing the climate to get warmer.

2 Research has shown that the modern day lifestyle is contributing to climate change as greenhouse gases are released when we burn fuels such as gas, coal and oil for energy. However, there is plenty that can be done to decrease the volume of greenhouse gases we produce and slow the process of global warming – for example, by using renewable energy resources and **1** making sure that homes and businesses are as energy efficient as possible.

| **1** | Home owners and businesses are already working towards being more energy efficient. |

Correct answer is C: Cannot say – you can see from the highlighted text in the final paragraph of the verbal information that there are measures that can be taken by homes and businesses, but there is no specific information about whether these measures are already being taken – it would be wrong to infer either way. Because of this uncertainty from the information given the correct answer is Cannot say.

| **2** | Our lifestyle has no connection with climate change. |

Correct answer is B: False – you can see that the statement is false in the highlighted text in the final paragraph – our lifestyle contributes to global warming according to research.

| **3** | The greenhouse effect has global consequences. |

Correct answer is A: True – you can see that the statement is true in the highlighted text in the second paragraph of the verbal information – a consequence of the greenhouse effect is a rise in global temperatures.

| **4** | In the future the sea level will be higher than it is now. |

Correct answer is A: True – you can see that the statement is true in the highlighted text in the first paragraph of the verbal information – a rise in sea levels is a consequence of climate change, meaning sea levels will continue to rise, causing the sea level to be higher than it is now.

| **5** | Climate change is the only environmental issue people need to be concerned about. |

Correct answer is B: False – you can see that the statement is false in the highlighted text in the first paragraph – climate change is the single biggest issue but not the only environmental issue we face.

How did you do?

Score of 5	Score of 4	Score of 3	Score of 2	Score of 1
Great performance	Good performance	Average performance	Below average performance	Poor performance

THE E-SLAB – WIREDFORSOUND EXCLUSIVE UK DEAL

Rob Gordon, the founder of the **Wiredforsound** online retailer, has announced an exclusive deal to sell the new e-slab device in the UK, beating off bids from other retailers in a highly competitive fight for rights to sell the new 'must-have' product.

The e-slab is set to revolutionise the way we spend money on electronic products for the home by integrating features and functions that are already available in other devices we own into a single, slightly bigger machine.

Rob enthusiastically praised the e-slab. 'For the first time I have a single device for playing music, reading books, surfing the web and watching TV, which fits into a very large pocket.' Rob believes that the e-slab will empower people to replace the TVs, laptops, MP3 players and books they already own with a single, expensive device.

But many industry analysts question the likely popularity of the e-slab and the benefits it will bring to **Wiredforsound**'s business. One analyst commented, 'To achieve total market dominance the e-slab needs to be useful throughout the home; the addition of a tin-opener would be a step in the right direction.'

A	B	C
TRUE	**FALSE**	**CANNOT SAY**
Fill in **A** if the statement is **True** from the information given.	Fill in **B** if the statement is **False** from the information given.	Fill in **C** if you **Cannot say** for certain from the information given whether the statement is true or false.

1   Wiredforsound's bid for the e-slab was higher than the bids offered by its competitors.

Ⓐ	Ⓑ	Ⓒ
TRUE	FALSE	CANNOT SAY

2   Wiredforsound will be the only retailer to sell the e-slab in the UK.

Ⓐ	Ⓑ	Ⓒ
TRUE	FALSE	CANNOT SAY

3   The e-slab can do things that other electronic devices cannot.

Ⓐ	Ⓑ	Ⓒ
TRUE	FALSE	CANNOT SAY

4   People who buy the e-slab will want to replace all their existing devices.

Ⓐ	Ⓑ	Ⓒ
TRUE	FALSE	CANNOT SAY

5   The e-slab has a built-in tin-opener.

Ⓐ	Ⓑ	Ⓒ
TRUE	FALSE	CANNOT SAY

THE E-SLAB – WIREDFORSOUND EXCLUSIVE UK DEAL

Rob Gordon, the founder of the **Wiredforsound** online retailer, has announced an **2** exclusive deal to sell the new e-slab device in the UK, **1** beating off bids from other retailers in a highly competitive fight for rights to sell the new 'must-have' product.

The e-slab is set to revolutionise the way we spend money on electronic products for the home **3** by integrating features and functions that are already available in other devices we own into a single, slightly bigger machine.

Rob enthusiastically praised the e-slab. 'For the first time I have a single device for playing music, reading books, surfing the web and watching TV, which fits into a very large pocket.' Rob believes that **4** the e-slab will empower people to replace the TVs, laptops, MP3 players and books they already own with a single, expensive device.

But many industry analysts question the likely popularity of the e-slab and the benefits it will bring to **Wiredforsound**'s business. One analyst commented, 'To achieve total market dominance the e-slab needs to be useful throughout the home; **5** the addition of a tin-opener would be a step in the right direction.'

1   **Wiredforsound**'s bid for the e-slab was higher than the bids offered by its competitors.

Correct answer is C: Cannot say – you can see from the highlighted text in the first paragraph of the verbal information that **Wiredforsound**'s bid beat off bids from other retailers but it does not say that the bid was successful because it was higher. There is no specific information about why the bid was successful – it would be wrong to infer that it won because it was higher or worth more in some way. Because of this uncertainty from the information given the correct answer is Cannot say.

2   **Wiredforsound** will be the only retailer to sell the e-slab in the UK.

Correct answer is A: True – you can see that the statement is true in the highlighted text in the first line of the first paragraph of the verbal information – **Wiredforsound** has secured an exclusive UK deal to sell the device.

3   The e-slab can do things that other electronic devices cannot.

Correct answer is B: False – you can see that the statement is false in the highlighted text in the second paragraph – the e-slab incorporates features and functions that are already available in other devices – therefore, the e-slab is the only device to combine all of these features, but none of these features are unique to this device.

4   People who buy the e-slab will want to replace all their existing devices.

Correct answer is C: Cannot say – the highlighted text in the third paragraph of the verbal information describes Rob's belief that the e-slab will empower people to replace the TVs, laptops, MP3 players and books they already own. This is not the same as saying that people will want to replace them; buying the e-slab will simply allow them to do so if they choose. So we can infer from the information that some people may want to replace their existing devices and some will not. We therefore cannot say for certain that everyone who buys an e-slab will want to replace all their existing devices. The correct answer is Cannot say.

5   The e-slab has a built in tin-opener.

Correct answer is B: False – the highlighted text in the final paragraph describes an analyst's view that a tin-opener should be added to the e-slab in order for it to be truly successful. The e-slab does not therefore currently have a tin-opener built in and so the correct answer is False.

How did you do?

Score of 5	Score of 4	Score of 3	Score of 2	Score of 1
Great performance	Good performance	Average performance	Below average performance	Poor performance

WHAT ARE PSYCHOMETRIC TESTS?

Psychometric tests make reliable and accurate measurements of the mental properties of the individual. The mental properties measured by occupational psychometric tests are generally attributes that are important to success in the job for which candidates are being selected. Because the results of psychometric tests are reliable we are able to use them to make predictions of performance in the job.

Psychometric tests can measure a range of mental properties including verbal, numerical, mechanical and spatial reasoning abilities. Psychometric instruments can also measure personality, attitudes and motivations.

Psychometric tests typically consist of a number of test items (questions or statements), which are administered to candidates under standardised conditions. There are usually a lot of items in a test because this makes the test more reliable and accurate.

Psychometric tests are generally very reliable but not infallible. One of the biggest sources of error in testing is the administration session. This is why it is essential that tests are administered in a professional and standardised way.

A	B	C
TRUE	**FALSE**	**CANNOT SAY**
Fill in **A** if the statement is **True** from the information given.	Fill in **B** if the statement is **False** from the information given.	Fill in **C** if you **Cannot say** for certain from the information given whether the statement is true or false.

1 Psychometric tests measure verbal ability accurately and reliably.

(A)	(B)	(C)
TRUE	FALSE	CANNOT SAY

2 Verbal ability is likely to be a valuable attribute for success in jobs.

(A)	(B)	(C)
TRUE	FALSE	CANNOT SAY

3 The length of a test does not affect how reliable or accurate it will be.

(A)	(B)	(C)
TRUE	FALSE	CANNOT SAY

4 Psychometrics that measure personality are less accurate than ability tests.

(A)	(B)	(C)
TRUE	FALSE	CANNOT SAY

5 If a test is administered badly it will make more errors.

(A)	(B)	(C)
TRUE	FALSE	CANNOT SAY

WHAT ARE PSYCHOMETRIC TESTS?

1 **Psychometric tests make reliable and accurate measurements** of the mental properties of the individual. The **2** **mental properties measured by occupational psychometric tests are generally attributes that are important to success in the job** for which candidates are being selected. Because the results of psychometric tests are reliable we are able to use them to make predictions of performance in the job.

Psychometric tests can **1** **2** **measure a range of mental properties including verbal**, numerical, mechanical and spatial reasoning abilities. **4** **Psychometric instruments can also measure personality, attitudes and motivations**.

Psychometric tests typically consist of a number of test items (questions or statements), which are administered to candidates under standardised conditions. **3** **There are usually a lot of items in a test because this makes the test more reliable and accurate**.

Psychometric tests are generally **5** **very reliable but not infallible. One of the biggest sources of error in testing is the administration session**. This is why it is essential that tests are administered in a professional and standardised way.

1	Psychometric tests measure verbal ability accurately and reliably.

Correct answer is A: True – You need to put two pieces of information from the passage together in order to answer this question. The first line of the first paragraph states that psychometric tests measure mental properties accurately and reliably. The first line of the second paragraph states that verbal ability is among the mental properties that psychometric tests can measure. We can therefore infer that the statement is true because the passage tells us that verbal ability is one of the mental properties that psychometric tests measure and that they do so in a reliable and accurate fashion.

2	Verbal ability is likely to be a valuable attribute for success in jobs.

Correct answer is A: True – Once again you need to infer the correct answer from more than one piece of information in the extract. The second line of the first paragraph states that psychometric tests measure mental properties that are generally attributes which are important to success in the job. The first line of the second paragraph states that verbal ability is among the mental properties that psychometric tests can measure. We can therefore infer that the statement is true because the passage tells us that psychometric tests tend to measure things that are valuable job attributes and that verbal ability is one of the mental properties that psychometric tests measure.

3	The length of a test does not affect how reliable or accurate it will be.

Correct answer is B: False – You can see that the final sentence of the third paragraph states that there are usually a lot of items in a test because this makes the test more reliable and accurate. We can therefore deduce that longer tests are more reliable and accurate because the more items a test contains the more reliable it will be. The correct answer is therefore False.

4	Psychometrics that measure personality are less accurate than ability tests.

Correct answer is C: Cannot say – the highlighted text at the end of the second paragraph states that psychometric instruments can also measure personality. No information is given about the relative reliability of a personality instrument compared with an ability test. The correct answer is therefore Cannot say.

5	If a test is administered badly it will make more errors.

Correct answer is A: True – We can see this statement is true in the final paragraph, which describes how tests are not infallible and that a big factor in making them less than 100% reliable is error in the test administration session. The passage tells us that this can be avoided through correct and professional administration of the test. We can deduce that correct administration of the test reduces error and therefore poor administration would increase errors. The statement is therefore true based on the information given.

How did you do?

Score of 5	Score of 4	Score of 3	Score of 2	Score of 1
Great performance	Good performance	Average performance	Below average performance	Poor performance

A CHANGE OF PACE FOR
THE FINAL PRACTICE TEST

Well done for working through the first nine verbal reasoning tests. These mid-level practice tests are representative of the most commonly used form of verbal ability tests because they reflect the verbal ability demands
of the widest range of jobs.

There is one more verbal reasoning test and it is a little different from the previous nine practice tests. The test uses the usual format applied by modern occupational tests of verbal ability – it has a passage of verbal information followed by some multiple-choice questions. This time though the test uses a range of multiple-choice formats.

We've varied the format so that you can see that while the formats may vary, the approach you have developed over the course of your work so far need not. The practice and skills you have developed will transfer seamlessly to the other formats.

INSTRUCTIONS FOR PRACTICE TEST 10

The instructions for this test are identical to the previous practice tests. You should read the verbal information and then evaluate each of the questions about the text. For each question you must pick the answer you think is correct from the options given. You must base your answers on the information given.

This test contains six questions and you should allow yourself six minutes to complete it.

OPTIMISM IN ADVERSITY

Optimism and confidence among the UK business professionals remains high despite the recession, according to research conducted by business psychologists.

The survey of 776 UK business professionals revealed that more than two thirds (68%) of UK professionals feel optimistic about the short-term future of their business.

When describing their personal perceptions of the prospects for their businesses, the majority of respondents (68%) felt optimistic about the short-term economic future of their business (within the next 12 months), and an even greater number (76%) reported optimism about the medium to long-term future (between one and five years).

In addition, the majority of respondents reported that there had been no effect on recruitment, training and employee-welfare budgets as a result of the recession.

Alan Redman, business psychologist with Criterion Partnership Ltd, comments: 'We found that the vast majority of business people feel optimistic about the short, medium and long-term prospects of their businesses. Despite regular, negative news concerning the credit crunch and its effects, the prevailing mood among the business people surveyed was characterised by resilience, confidence and optimism. Successful businesses are those which capitalise on the optimism and resilience of their staff in the face of economic adversity.'

These survey results suggest a disconnection between current economic conditions, media predictions and the psychological mindset among people working in business.

> **1** Optimism among business people has not been affected by the recession.

A. The statement is **True from** the information given.
B. The statement is **False from** the information given.
C. You **Cannot say** for certain from the information given whether the statement is true or false.

> **2** Which of these statements most accurately reflects the results of the survey?

A. There is an even split between optimism and pessimism among UK professionals.
B. UK professionals feel optimistic about their immediate business prospects.
C. UK professionals feel more optimistic about the short-term than the long-term future.
D. UK professionals are more optimistic than they were before the recession.

> **3** Which of these statements most accurately reflects the beliefs of the business psychologist?

A. Negative news reporting about the recession has created pessimism among people in business.
B. Newspapers should avoid printing bad news.
C. People don't pay attention to bad news reported by the media.
D. Negative news reporting about the recession has not affected optimism among people in business.

> **4** To be successful businesses must draw on the emotional strength of their employees.

A. The statement is **True** from the information given.
B. The statement is **False** from the information given.
C. You **Cannot say** for certain from the information given whether the statement is true or false.

> **5** Which of these words would best replace 'prevailing' in this statement without changing the meaning of the passage? *The **prevailing** mood among the business people surveyed was characterised by resilience, confidence and optimism.*

A. Favourite   C. Minority
B. Dominant   D. Consistent

> **6** Which of these statements most accurately reflects the results of the survey?

A. The recession has affected recruitment, training and employee-welfare budgets.
B. There is a link between optimism and budgets for recruitment, training and employee-welfare
C. Recruitment, training and employee-welfare budgets have not changed.
D. Recruitment, training and employee-welfare budgets are immune to the effects of a recession.

OPTIMISM IN ADVERSITY

1 **Optimism and confidence among the UK business professionals remains high despite the recession**, according to research conducted by business psychologists.

The survey of 776 UK business professionals revealed that **2** **more than two-thirds (68%) of UK professionals feel optimistic about the short-term future of their business**.

When describing their personal perceptions of the prospects for their businesses, the majority of respondents (68%) felt optimistic about the short-term economic future of their business (within the next 12 months), and an even greater number (76%) reported optimism about the medium to long-term future (between one and five years).

In addition, the majority of respondents reported that there had been **6** **no effect on recruitment, training and employee-welfare budgets as a result of the recession.**

Alan Redman, business psychologist with Criterion Partnership Ltd, comments: 'We found that the vast majority of business people feel optimistic about the short, medium and long-term prospects of their businesses. **3** **Despite regular, negative news concerning the credit crunch and its effects, the prevailing mood among the business people surveyed was characterised by resilience, confidence and optimism.** **4** **Successful businesses are those which capitalise on the optimism and resilience of their staff in the face of economic adversity.**'

These survey results suggest a disconnection between current economic conditions, media predictions and the psychological mindset among people working in business.

| **1** | Optimism among business people has not been affected by the recession. |

Correct answer is C: Cannot say The highlighted text in the first paragraph states that optimism and confidence among the UK business professionals remains high despite the recession. Optimism levels could be at a reduced level compared to where they were before the recession and still be high. We cannot say for certain whether optimism has been unchanged by the recession or not; we simply know that it is high. The correct answer is therefore Cannot say.

| **2** | Which of these statements most accurately reflects the results of the survey? |

The correct answer is: B UK professionals feel optimistic about their immediate business prospects. You can see the highlighted text in the second paragraph states that over two-thirds of UK professionals feel optimistic about the short-term future of their business. None of the other statements in this question are supported by the information in the passage.

| **3** | Which of these statements most accurately reflects the beliefs of the business psychologist? |

The correct answer is: D Negative news reporting about the recession has not affected optimism among people in business. The highlighted text in the fifth paragraph describes the psychologist's view that business people feel good despite the negative news. Statement A is wrong and statements B and C infer meaning that is not stated in the passage.

| **4** | To be successful businesses must draw on the emotional strength of their employees. |

Correct answer is A: True – highlighted text at the end of the fifth paragraph describes the psychologist's conclusion that it is the optimism and resilience of staff that help businesses survive a recession.

| **5** | Which of these words would best replace 'prevailing' in this statement without changing the meaning of the passage? *The prevailing mood among the business people surveyed was characterised by resilience, confidence and optimism.* |

Correct answer is B: Dominant. None of the other words accurately capture the meaning of this part of the passage, which describes how these positive emotions were the most common found among business people surveyed.

| **6** | Which of these statements most accurately reflects the results of the survey? |

Correct answer is C: Recruitment, training and employee-welfare budgets have not changed. The highlighted text in the fourth paragraph states that there has been no effect on recruitment, training and employee-welfare budgets as a result of the recession. None of the other statements in this question are supported by the information in the passage.

How did you do?

Score of 6	Score of 5	Score of 3–4	Score of 2	Score of 1
Great performance	Good performance	Average performance	Below average performance	Poor performance

TOTAL SCORES: RATE YOUR PERFORMANCE

These practice tests are too short individually to make an accurate measurement of your verbal reasoning ability, but if you put your results together we can provide a clearer view. Add the scores from each of the 10 practice tests together and compare your total score with the table below to gauge your performance.

Total score	What it means	Advice for further development
50+	Excellent performance	It looks like you're pretty much there in terms of developing your personal best score. Don't rest on your laurels though. Make sure that you take the time to work through the next chapter of this book, which contains more challenging verbal-critical reasoning tests. Completing these more difficult questions will give you an opportunity to stretch your verbal ability to its maximum level. It will also make you feel more confident when next faced with a more straightforward, mid-level, verbal reasoning test. Make sure you work through the chapters at the end of the book as well – they will provide you with more valuable preparation for performing well at verbal tests.
40–49	Good performance	This level of performance should see you through most verbal tests at this level; but if you feel that it does not reflect your potential personal best score then you might want to do some more practice. Review the advice in Chapter 2 about test strategies and practice advice and then have another go at these practice questions.

Total score	What it means	Advice for further development
30–39	Average performance	Verbal reasoning tests are the most widely used level of verbal assessment so an average score is still a positive result. However, you could benefit from doing some more work to practise and pass verbal tests at this level more effortlessly. Review the advice in Chapter 2 about test strategies and practising advice. You can also review your wrong answers to the practice questions to try and identify any trends in where you go wrong. It might be that the harder 'cannot say' answers give you the most trouble. Whatever the case, spend some time reviewing where you went wrong and then attempt the practice questions again.
20–29	Below average performance	These are mid-level tests so you might want to polish your verbal ability by correcting any shortfalls in your verbal comprehension abilities by revisiting your work in Chapter 3. Once you are happy that your performance at those foundation level tests reflects your true potential you should return to these verbal reasoning tests. To begin with do not apply the time-limits when you attempt these mid-level tests – and see if that makes a difference. If time is a factor then you should identify which areas of your test-taking strategy might be letting you down. Spend some time developing and exercising your raw verbal ability through reading, solving puzzles and taking part in discussions alongside further practice from this book.
0–19	Low performance	

Remember that these 10 practice tests are pitched at the level of difficulty you are most likely to be tested at in the workplace. Verbal tests at this level are often used alongside tests of other abilities, such as numerical reasoning. It's a good idea to balance your performance across different tests so that you can maximise your overall results. Consider working through other books in the *Practice & Pass* series to help you develop all your strengths.

CHAPTER 5
VERBAL CRITICAL-REASONING

Verbal critical-reasoning tests are the most advanced form of verbal test. These tests contain complex and high-level verbal information that is designed to simulate the demands of senior level jobs.

The questions are designed to assess your ability to draw conclusions and make complex decisions about the verbal information in the test. These decisions sometimes require you to use inference or deal with ambiguity in the information.

These practice questions are equivalent to those in real verbal critical-reasoning tests – the only difference being that in the real test there would be more verbal information and questions and a longer time limit.

GETTING THE MOST FROM THESE PRACTICE QUESTIONS

These verbal critical-reasoning practice questions are grouped together into 10 short practice tests. Each practice test mirrors the approach of a real test: there is a short extract of verbal information followed by a series of five questions for you to answer about the information you have read.

The test instructions for these practice tests follow the same format and approach of instructions in real tests – so make sure that you familiarise yourself with these so that you are more prepared when taking an actual test.

You are encouraged to complete each practice test one at a time and to spend time at the end of each short test to review your responses against the correct answers. Once you are happy with your work you can move on to the next test.

Completing the practice tests

Ideally you should complete the practice tests in conditions that are as close to the real testing environment and experience as possible.

▶ Find a quiet place that is free from any distractions.
▶ Read the practice test instructions before beginning the first practice test.
▶ Real tests have strict time limits. Simulate this by giving yourself seven minutes per practice test. Start timing from the point you begin reading the verbal information for the test.
▶ Mark your answers in the spaces provided beneath each practice question by fully colouring in the circle for the answer you think is correct.
▶ Do not turn over to the correct answers until you have completed all the practice questions.

Advice for verbal critical-reasoning tests

Remember that verbal critical-reasoning tests are the most difficult of all verbal tests. When completing a verbal critical-reasoning test, remember these points to perform at your personal best.

Read the verbal information carefully before beginning the practice questions. You do not need to memorise it but you will perform better if you are familiar with the information when attempting the questions.

Never simply write down your answer without checking it first. When you think you know the answer to a question straightaway you should always check your understanding by rereading the pertinent part of the verbal information to make sure you are not mistaken.

Watch out for traps. With verbal critical reasoning tests it is important to know where the test author is tempting you to answer on the basis of assumption or outside knowledge. Remember to base your answers on the information given. Ignore anything you understand to be true or false in the real world.

Use any time remaining to check your answers. If you complete all five questions in a practice test within the seven minutes time-limit you should recheck your answers, as you would in a real test. This is good test-taking strategy and you should aim to make it a habit.

If you have jumped straight to these practice tests without completing the lower level verbal tests and verbal reasoning tests we encourage you to stop and go back. Completing the easier tests in turn will greatly benefit your test-taking strategies and level of practice.

Before you begin the practice tests

Read the test instructions carefully before you begin. These instructions have been adapted from real test instructions. When you take a real test you will be presented with instructions that follow this format – so take time to benefit from great familiarity with the language and information they include.

Reviewing your answers

Once you have completed a practice test you can turn over the page to check your responses against the correct answers. Along with each correct answer we have provided some additional help and explanation about the answer. We have also highlighted the text within the verbal information that relates to the correct answer.

These practice tests are too short to make an accurate measurement of your verbal critical-reasoning ability (that's what real tests are for), but we can provide some guidance about what your results mean:

Score of 5	Score of 4	Score of 3	Score of 2	Score of 1
Great performance	Good performance	Average performance	Below average performance	Poor performance

If you have scored less than your ideal personal best score then you should look at the pattern of your responses – do you tend to answer specific types of question incorrectly? With verbal critical-reasoning tests it is often the 'cannot say' questions that cause people the most trouble. Below is some advice for improving your performance against each of the response types.

Is the correct answer true?	Before answering 'true' check your answer by identifying the text in the verbal information that confirms that the statement is true.
Is the correct answer false?	Before answering 'false' check your answer by identifying the text in the verbal information that confirms that the statement is false.
Is the correct answer cannot say?	If you cannot find any text in the verbal information that definitively tells you the statement is true or false then you cannot say.

You can also use this as a process for answering questions that you find difficult when you are taking a real test by working through each of the three points to identify the correct answer.

Once you have reviewed your answers take a short break before attempting the next test.

VERBAL CRITICAL-REASONING PRACTICE TESTS

PRACTICE TEST INSTRUCTIONS

These practice tests each consist of five questions
that relate to verbal information given on the first page of each
test. You are required to use this verbal information to evaluate the
statements that are presented next to the text. You should mark
your answers in the spaces provided below each of the questions
by filling in the appropriate circle, A, B, or C according to these
rules:

(A) TRUE	(B) FALSE	(C) CANNOT SAY
Fill in **A** if the statement is **True** from the information given.	Fill in **B** if the statement is **False** from the information given.	Fill in **C** if you **Cannot say** for certain from the information given whether the statement is true or false.

These rules are repeated above the statements. In order to arrive
at your answers use only the verbal information given on the facing
page of each test. **Assume that this given information is correct,
even if it contradicts what you believe to be the case in reality.**

▶ Allow yourself a seven-minute time-limit for each of the
  practice tests.
▶ You should work quickly and accurately.
▶ If you are not sure of an answer, fill in what you think the
  right answer is, but do not simply guess your answers.
▶ Check your answers against the correct answers given on
  the pages that follow each practice test.

Remember these important points:

▶ Complete each practice test in a quiet place that is free from any distractions.

▶ Start timing the practice test from the point you begin reading the verbal information.

▶ Mark your answers in the spaces provided beneath each practice question by fully colouring in the circle for the answer you think is correct.

▶ Do not turn over to the correct answers until you have completed all the practice questions.

Please turn over to the first practice test, start timing yourself and read through the verbal information now. You should then start answering the questions as soon as you are ready.

WELCOME TO *UTOPIA!* THE MAGAZINE FOR THE FUTURE

Utopia Magazine is now established as Britain's most influential ecology orientated magazine. Its circulation has risen steadily every year since its launch seven years ago and now equals that of the most popular women's fashion magazines.

Utopia Magazine tells you what is happening on your planet now. We were the first to publish government figures on North Sea pollution. We were also a major catalyst for creating world-wide awareness of the hole in the ozone layer.

Utopia Magazine also provides helpful and practical information on natural health issues. Past features span from reflexology and nutrition to meditation and natural family planning!

Utopia Magazine's talented and forward-thinking editorial team has been drawn from all over the world. Our Japanese art director was previously the art editor of *Visage* magazine and we are very proud to have Margaret Shymer as our new editor. Margaret spent many years as the editor of America's *Living* magazine, then helped to establish the 'green movement' in the UK, before coming to *Utopia Magazine*.

Utopia Magazine is printed on recycled paper and we make use of the most advanced technology in the printing processes to ensure that wastage in minimised. *Utopia Magazine* is published monthly at a cover price of £2.50.

A	B	C
TRUE	**FALSE**	**CANNOT SAY**
Fill in **A** if the statement is **True** from the information given.	Fill in **B** if the statement is **False** from the information given.	Fill in **C** if you **Cannot say** for certain from the information given whether the statement is true or false.

1 *Utopia Magazine* covers issues which relate to ecology.

(A)	(B)	(C)
TRUE	FALSE	CANNOT SAY

2 *Utopia Magazine's* editorial policy has always excluded issues which are not directly related to pollution of the environment.

(A)	(B)	(C)
TRUE	FALSE	CANNOT SAY

3 *Utopia Magazine's* editorial staff have acquired previous experience with some of the world's top magazine titles.

(A)	(B)	(C)
TRUE	FALSE	CANNOT SAY

4 *Utopia Magazine's* editor has previous experience of working with environmental issues.

(A)	(B)	(C)
TRUE	FALSE	CANNOT SAY

5 *Utopia Magazine* published government figures on the hole in the ozone layer.

(A)	(B)	(C)
TRUE	FALSE	CANNOT SAY

WELCOME TO *UTOPIA!* THE MAGAZINE FOR THE FUTURE

Utopia Magazine is now established as Britain's most influential **1 ecology orientated magazine**. Its circulation has risen steadily every year since its launch seven years ago and now equals that of the most popular women's fashion magazines.

Utopia Magazine tells you what is happening on your planet now. We were the first to publish government figures on North Sea pollution. **5 We were also a major catalyst for creating world-wide awareness of the hole in the ozone layer.**

2 *Utopia Magazine* **also provides helpful and practical information on natural health issues. Past features span from reflexology and nutrition to meditation and natural family planning!**

Utopia Magazine's talented and forward-thinking editorial team has been drawn from all over the world. **3 Our Japanese art director was previously the art editor of** *Visage* **magazine and we are very proud to have Margaret Shymer as our new editor**. Margaret spent many years as the editor of America's *Living* magazine, then **4 helped to establish the 'green movement' in the UK**, before coming to *Utopia Magazine*.

Utopia Magazine is printed on recycled paper and we make use of the most advanced technology in the printing processes to ensure that wastage in minimised. *Utopia Magazine* is published monthly at a cover price of £2.50.

1   *Utopia Magazine* covers issues which relate to ecology.

Correct answer is A: True – you can see that the statement is true in the highlighted text in the first line of the verbal information.

2   *Utopia Magazine*'s editorial policy has always excluded issues which are not directly related to pollution of the environment.

Correct answer is B: False – you can see that the statement is false in the highlighted text in the third paragraph of the verbal information – *Utopia Magazine* covers a range of non-environmental subjects.

3   *Utopia Magazine*'s editorial staff have acquired previous experience with some of the world's top magazine titles.

Correct answer is C: Cannot say – you can see from the highlighted text in the fourth paragraph that some of *Utopia Magazine*'s editorial staff have previously worked for other magazines (such as *Visage* and *Living*) but nothing is stated about these being among the world's top magazine titles. We cannot say whether the statement is true or false – it might be either, so the correct answer is Cannot say.

4   *Utopia Magazine*'s editor has previous experience of working with environmental issues.

Correct answer is A: True – you can see that the statement is true in the highlighted text in the fourth paragraph – she helped to establish the 'green movement' in the UK before working with *Utopia Magazine*.

5   *Utopia Magazine* published government figures on the hole in the ozone layer.

Correct answer is C: Cannot say – you can see from the highlighted text in the second paragraph that *Utopia Magazine* helped create awareness of the ozone layer issue but no mention is given about its role in publishing government figures. The correct answer is Cannot say because while we can't say it's true, we also can't say for certain that it is false from the information given – *Utopia Magazine* may have published the figures but we don't know for certain. This is a good example of why care must be taken before answering true or false – always check what the verbal information says (or doesn't say!).

How did you do?

Score of 5	Score of 4	Score of 3	Score of 2	Score of 1
Great performance	Good performance	Average performance	Below average performance	Poor performance

PROTECTING OUR PLANET – *UTOPIA MAGAZINE* ONLINE

Utopia Online is the UK's favourite environmental website, linked to *Utopia Magazine* – Britain's most influential publication on green issues.

Utopia Online tells you what is happening on your planet **now**. Our aims are to raise awareness on environmental concerns, to provide practical advice on caring for our natural world, and to sustain pressure on governments, corporations and individuals to act responsibly for the long-term protection of the planet.

Visits to **Utopia Online** have risen steadily every year since its launch five years ago.

This week's key updates cover:

▶ wildlife diversity – European progress on protecting nature
▶ climate change – Arctic melt has doubled in 10 years
▶ through the roof – reducing carbon dioxide emissions through loft insulation
▶ driving me crazy – some facts about the UK's motoring mania
▶ natural foods – healthy eating for a harmonious society
▶ rainwater harvesting – new thinking on averting international drought.

A	B	C
TRUE	**FALSE**	**CANNOT SAY**
Fill in **A** if the statement is **True** from the information given.	Fill in **B** if the statement is **False** from the information given.	Fill in **C** if you **Cannot say** for certain from the information given whether the statement is true or false.

1 Utopia Online aims to protect the environment through a mix of awareness, advice and pressure.

Ⓐ	Ⓑ	Ⓒ
TRUE	FALSE	CANNOT SAY

2 The **Utopia Online** website is wholly owned by *Utopia Magazine*.

Ⓐ	Ⓑ	Ⓒ
TRUE	FALSE	CANNOT SAY

3 Visits to the **Utopia Online** website dropped between the second and third year after its launch.

Ⓐ	Ⓑ	Ⓒ
TRUE	FALSE	CANNOT SAY

4 Utopia Online advocates individual responsibility, alongside corporate and political governance.

Ⓐ	Ⓑ	Ⓒ
TRUE	FALSE	CANNOT SAY

5 *Utopia Magazine* is Britain's best-selling environmental magazine.

Ⓐ	Ⓑ	Ⓒ
TRUE	FALSE	CANNOT SAY

PROTECTING OUR PLANET – *UTOPIA MAGAZINE* ONLINE

Utopia Online is the UK's favourite environmental website, **2** **linked to *Utopia Magazine* –** **5** **Britain's most influential publication** on green issues.

Utopia Online tells you what is happening on your planet **now**. Our aims are to **1** **raise awareness on environmental concerns, to provide practical advice on caring for our natural world, and** **4** **to sustain pressure on governments, corporations and individuals to act responsibly for the long-term protection of the planet.**

3 **Visits to Utopia Online have risen steadily every year since its launch five years ago.**

This week's key updates cover:

▶ Wildlife diversity – European progress on protecting nature
▶ Climate change – Arctic melt has doubled in 10 years
▶ Through the roof – reducing carbon dioxide emissions through loft insulation
▶ Driving me crazy – some facts about the UK's motoring mania
▶ Natural foods – healthy eating for a harmonious society
▶ Rainwater harvesting – new thinking on averting international drought

1	**Utopia Online** aims to protect the environment through a mix of awareness, advice and pressure.

Correct answer is A: True – you can see that the statement is true in the highlighted text in the second paragraph of the verbal information.

2	The **Utopia Online** website is wholly owned by *Utopia Magazine*.

Correct answer is C: Cannot say – you can see from the highlighted text in the first paragraph that Utopia Online is **linked** to *Utopia Magazine*. While you could infer or assume that Utopia Online is therefore owned by *Utopia Magazine*, **we cannot be certain**. The correct answer is therefore Cannot say. This is a prime example of a verbal critical-reasoning test question that requires you to avoid making assumptions based on your understanding of what you've read.

3	Visits to the **Utopia Online** website dropped between the second and third year after its launch.

Correct answer is B: False – you can see that the statement is false in the highlighted text in the third paragraph of the verbal information – visits have risen steadily every year.

4	**Utopia Online** advocates individual responsibility, alongside corporate and political governance.

Correct answer is A: True – you can see that the statement is true in the highlighted text in the second paragraph of the verbal information – *Utopia Magazine* sustains pressure on individuals as well governments and corporations to take responsibility for the environment.

5	*Utopia Magazine* is Britain's best selling environmental magazine.

Correct answer is C: Cannot say – you can see from the highlighted text in the first paragraph that *Utopia Magazine* is the most influential environmental magazine. The correct answer is therefore Cannot say because we cannot assume that being the most influential magazine makes it the best-selling – we would need extra information to know for certain. This is another example of a verbal critical-reasoning test question that requires you to avoid making assumptions.

How did you do?

Score of 5	Score of 4	Score of 3	Score of 2	Score of 1
Great performance	Good performance	Average performance	Below average performance	Poor performance

LOSING MY EMISSIONS – THE FUTURE OF GREEN MOTORING

Do catalytic converters prevent pollution?

While catalytic converters don't actually prevent pollution, they do help to cut it down. Their purpose is to convert the poisonous carbon monoxide gas, and other pollutants produced by cars, into carbon dioxide. They don't, however, work to full effect on short car journeys since they only work once they have been warmed up.

Are electric cars greener?

This is entirely dependent on how the electricity is generated. The electricity generated from the burning of coal, for example, is likely to have high emissions of pollution. On the other hand, electricity generated by nuclear power will have less emissions of harmful gases than an ordinary petrol or diesel car. Electric cars are also problematic because they need heavy and expensive batteries which need to be frequently recharged. They are not so good for travelling long distances.

Is diesel a cleaner fuel than petrol?

This is a complicated issue because the emissions produced by a diesel car are different to those produced by a petrol car, and much depends on how well a car is maintained. Some diesel cars might actually give off more harmful gases than petrol cars.

Is it better for the environment to use biofuels?

This is not really true because they give off less energy per quantity than ordinary fuels. There is also the environmental cost of producing biofuels: intensive farming of the crops, fertilisers and pesticides used on them, and then the conversion of the crops into the fuels. Biofuels emit less sulphur than conventional fuels, but they do produce more nitrogen monoxide. Biofuels can have a negative effect on the environment.

What about future developments in fuel technology?

Hydrogen is often cited as the way forward for green motoring, with fuel-cell technology producing only water as a waste product. Although hydrogen is the most common element in the universe it requires complex processes for its production, storage and distribution. Nuclear-powered cars are really only suitable for time travel (which requires 1.21 gigawatts of electricity).

A	B	C
TRUE	**FALSE**	**CANNOT SAY**
Fill in **A** if the statement is **True** from the information given.	Fill in **B** if the statement is **False** from the information given.	Fill in **C** if you **Cannot say** for certain from the information given whether the statement is true or false.

1 Catalytic converters are most effective in reducing pollution when cars are used for short journeys.

Ⓐ	Ⓑ	Ⓒ
TRUE	FALSE	CANNOT SAY

2 Diesel cars generally emit smaller quantities of harmful gases than petrol cars.

Ⓐ	Ⓑ	Ⓒ
TRUE	FALSE	CANNOT SAY

3 Cars without catalytic converters produce poisonous substances.

Ⓐ	Ⓑ	Ⓒ
TRUE	FALSE	CANNOT SAY

4 On balance, biofuels are more environmentally safe than ordinary fuels.

Ⓐ	Ⓑ	Ⓒ
TRUE	FALSE	CANNOT SAY

5 There is an abundant supply of hydrogen available.

Ⓐ	Ⓑ	Ⓒ
TRUE	FALSE	CANNOT SAY

LOSING MY EMISSIONS – THE FUTURE OF GREEN MOTORING

Do catalytic converters prevent pollution?
Whilst catalytic converters don't actually prevent pollution, they do help to cut it down. Their purpose is to **3** **convert the poisonous carbon monoxide gas, and other pollutants produced by cars into carbon dioxide.** **1** **They don't, however, work to full effect on short car journeys since they only work once they have been warmed up.**

Are electric cars greener?
This is entirely dependent on how the electricity is generated. The electricity generated from the burning of coal, for example, is likely to have high emissions of pollution. On the other hand, electricity generated by nuclear power will have less emissions of harmful gases than an ordinary petrol or diesel car. Electric cars are also problematic because they need heavy and expensive batteries which need to be frequently recharged. They are not so good for travelling long distances.

Is diesel a cleaner fuel than petrol?
This is a complicated issue because the emissions produced by a diesel car are different to those produced by a petrol car, and much depends on how well a car is maintained. **2** **Some diesel cars might actually give off more harmful gases than petrol cars.**

Is it better for the environment to use biofuels?
This is not really true because **4** **they give off less energy per quantity than ordinary fuels.** There is also the **environmental cost of producing biofuels:** intensive farming of the crops, fertilisers and pesticides used on them, and then the conversion of the crops into the fuels. Biofuels emit less sulphur than conventional fuels, but they do **4** **produce more nitrogen monoxide. Biofuels can have a negative effect on the environment.**

What about future developments in fuel technology?
Hydrogen is often cited as the way forward for green motoring, with fuel-cell technology producing only water as a waste product. Although **5** **hydrogen is the most common element in the universe** it requires complex processes for its production, storage and distribution. Nuclear-powered cars are really only suitable for time travel (which requires 1.21 gigawatts of electricity).

1 Catalytic converters are most effective in reducing pollution when cars are used for short journeys.

Correct answer is B: False – you can see that the statement is false in the highlighted text at the end of the first paragraph of the verbal information, which clearly states that they are not fully effective for short journeys.

2 Diesel cars generally emit smaller quantities of harmful gases than petrol cars.

Correct answer is C: Cannot say – you can see from the highlighted text in the third paragraph that some diesel cars **might** actually give off more harmful gases than petrol cars; however this information does not state for certain that they definitely emit larger quantities of harmful gases. While the verbal information suggests that the statement is false, the correct answer is Cannot say because there is no definite statement of fact, only a 'might'. This is a good example of a verbal critical-reasoning test question that tests your ability to avoid forming an incorrect inference from incomplete information. This question is also a good example of a statement that tempts you to base your answer on what you know to be true in the real world – that diesel engines produce greater quantities of harmful particulates than petrol engines.

3 Cars without catalytic converters produce poisonous substances.

Correct answer is A: True – you can see that the statement is true in the highlighted text in the second line of the first paragraph of the verbal information – catalytic converters change poisonous gases emitted by cars into less harmful ones. It therefore logically follows that cars without catalytic converters produce poisonous gases. This is an example of a verbal critical-reasoning question that requires you to perform logical inference to get to the correct answer.

4 On balance, biofuels are more environmentally safe than ordinary fuels.

Correct answer is B: False – you can see that the statement is false in the highlighted text in the fourth paragraph of the verbal information, which states that biofuels have a higher environmental cost to produce and concludes by saying that they emit more nitrogen monoxide and so can have a negative effect on the environment meaning they are not more environmentally safe than ordinary fuels.

5 There is an abundant supply of hydrogen available.

Correct answer is A: True – you can see that the statement is true in the highlighted text in the final paragraph of the verbal information.

How did you do?

Score of 5	Score of 4	Score of 3	Score of 2	Score of 1
Great performance	Good performance	Average performance	Below average performance	Poor performance

ANTARCTICA – HOLIDAY CHOICE FOR THE TWENTY-FIRST CENTURY?

The vast expanse of Antarctica, larger than the United States and Europe combined, is fast becoming the latest choice for tourists who long to experience its unique beauty and unusual wildlife. But will the impact of tourists be beneficial or detrimental? This is a question which worries environmentalists and scientists alike.

Its temperature hardly rises above −20 degrees Celsius, even during its summer, and in the winter the sun never rises. It might not sound like the ideal tourist spot, but more and more people want to experience the sensation of being among acres of snow and ice. They want to see for themselves the incredible spectacle of the millions of seabirds and penguins which breed there.

Antarctica is, however, more than just an unspoilt area of outstanding natural beauty, it also has an important effect on the world's climate, its enormous expanse impacting on the movement of tides and winds. It acts as an invaluable environment for scientists to study the planet, having almost laboratory-like conditions and excellent visibility unaffected by the problems of water vapour. It is the ideal location for keeping track of the ozone layer, for example.

This uniqueness also makes it delicate and the development of tourism must therefore be a source of considerable concern. The prospect of visitors necessitating the construction of banks, hotels and airports has worried environmentalists who feel that the ecosystems of the vulnerable wildlife may be irreversibly affected.

On the good side, however, tourism is a far more preferable and probably much less destructive prospect than mining, for example (which has recently been banned for at least 50 years), or even drilling for oil. The way tourism develops can be controlled in order to have the least possible effect. Enabling people to actually experience the reality of Antarctica might inspire them to take an interest in preserving and protecting it far more than just reading about it in magazines, or seeing it on the television.

Perhaps then, we should not be too quick to condemn tourism. We have, after all, come a long way since we spoilt the beaches of Spain. It could be that all that is required to prevent a potential problem is careful planning and the consideration which is needed to ensure the continued survival of the special nature of Antarctica.

A TRUE	B FALSE	C CANNOT SAY
Fill in **A** if the statement is **True** from the information given.	Fill in **B** if the statement is **False** from the information given.	Fill in **C** if you **Cannot say** for certain from the information given whether the statement is true or false.

1 Scientific study is not possible in the harsh climate of Antarctica.

(A) TRUE	(B) FALSE	(C) CANNOT SAY

2 The development of tourism cannot be managed or constrained.

(A) TRUE	(B) FALSE	(C) CANNOT SAY

3 Environmentalists agree on the likely implications of tourism for Antarctica.

(A) TRUE	(B) FALSE	(C) CANNOT SAY

4 The composition of animals and plants found in Antarctica cannot be found elsewhere in the world.

(A) TRUE	(B) FALSE	(C) CANNOT SAY

5 Antarctica is bigger than America.

(A) TRUE	(B) FALSE	(C) CANNOT SAY

ANTARCTICA – HOLIDAY CHOICE FOR THE TWENTY-FIRST CENTURY?

The vast expanse of **5** **Antarctica, larger than the United States and Europe combined**, is fast becoming the latest choice for tourists who long to experience its unique beauty and **4** **unusual wildlife**. But will the impact of tourists be beneficial or detrimental? **3** **This is a question which worries environmentalists and scientists alike.**

Its temperature hardly rises above −20 degrees Celsius, even during its summer, and in the winter the sun never rises. It might not sound like the ideal tourist spot, but more and more people want to experience the sensation of being amongst acres of snow and ice. They want to see for themselves, the incredible spectacle of the millions of seabirds and penguins which breed there.

Antarctica, is however, more than just an unspoilt area of outstanding natural beauty, it also has an important effect on the world's climate, its enormous expanse impacting on the movement of tides and winds. **1** **It acts as an invaluable environment for scientists to study the planet, having almost laboratory-like conditions and excellent visibility unaffected by the problems of water vapour.** It is the ideal location for keeping track of the ozone layer, for example.

This uniqueness also makes it delicate and the development of tourism must therefore be a source of considerable concern. The prospect of visitors necessitating the construction of banks, hotels and airports has **3** **worried environmentalists who feel that the ecosystems of the vulnerable wildlife may be irreversibly affected.**

On the good side, however, tourism is a far more preferable and probably much less destructive prospect than mining, for example (which has recently been banned for at least 50 years), or even drilling for oil. **2** **The way tourism develops can be controlled in order to have the least possible effect.** Enabling people to actually experience the reality of Antarctica might inspire them to take an interest in preserving and protecting it far more than just reading about it in magazines, or seeing it on the television.

Perhaps then, we should not be too quick to condemn tourism. We have, after all, come a long way since we spoilt the beaches of Spain. It could be that all that is required to prevent a potential problem is careful planning and the consideration which is needed to ensure the continued survival of the special nature of Antarctica.

| 1 | Scientific study is not possible in the harsh climate of Antarctica. |

Correct answer is B: False – you can see that the statement is false in the highlighted text in the third paragraph of the verbal information, which states that scientific enquiry is made easier by the conditions in the area.

| 2 | The development of tourism cannot be managed or constrained. |

Correct answer is B: False – you can see that the statement is false in the highlighted text in the fifth paragraph of the verbal information, which states that the way tourism develops can be controlled.

| 3 | Environmentalists agree on the likely implications of tourism for Antarctica. |

Correct answer is C: Cannot say – there are two pieces of information, highlighted in paragraphs 1 and 4, which describe environmentalists as worried. There is no information that specifically spells out any agreement between environmentalists. It would be wrong to assume that this statement is true or false from the information given, so the correct answer is therefore Cannot say.

| 4 | The composition of animals and plants found in Antarctica cannot be found elsewhere in the world. |

Correct answer is C: Cannot say – the wildlife is described as unusual in the first paragraph but we cannot say for certain from the information that it is unique to the area. While our knowledge about the real world could lead us to answer the question as true the correct answer in the context of the verbal information is Cannot say. .

| 5 | Antarctica is bigger than the United States. |

Correct answer is A: True – you can see that the statement is true in the highlighted text in the first line of the first paragraph of the verbal information – Antarctica is larger than the United States and Europe combined. This is an example of a verbal critical-reasoning question that requires you to perform logical inference to get to the correct answer. If it is larger than both the United States and Europe combined, it logically follows that it is bigger than the United States alone.

How did you do?

Score of 5	Score of 4	Score of 3	Score of 2	Score of 1
Great performance	Good performance	Average performance	Below average performance	Poor performance

SUPERMARKET FREEZERS COME IN FROM THE COLD

Most leading supermarkets have reacted to the high-profile campaign to minimise the use of plastic carrier bags by selling re-useable bags, no longer offering customers free plastic bags or charging for them. Environmentalists are critical of these actions, pointing out that by far the biggest source of environmental threat posed by supermarkets is not plastic bags but refrigeration.

A recent study showed that 30% of the environmentally damaging chemicals emitted by supermarkets are due to leakage from fridges and freezers. The gases commonly used in refrigeration units as a coolant are called HFCs (hydrofluorocarbons) and while they do not damage the ozone layer like the old fashioned CFC gases they do contribute to global warming.

Fridges and freezers leak HFC gases over time. The total leakage from supermarkets is equivalent to one billion car journeys to a supermarket or the production of 5.6 billion plastic bags.

Until now this issue has received far less attention than the less environmentally damaging issue of free plastic bags. But now the supermarket chain SuperStoreUK has announced plans to introduce new refrigeration technology into all its stores over the next five years. These new fridges and freezers use carbon dioxide and ammonia instead of HFCs and are therefore less harmful to the environment.

A	B	C
TRUE	**FALSE**	**CANNOT SAY**
Fill in **A** if the statement is **True** from the information given.	Fill in **B** if the statement is **False** from the information given.	Fill in **C** if you **Cannot say** for certain from the information given whether the statement is true or false.

1 Supermarkets accept the arguments of the campaign to minimise the use of free plastic carrier bags.

Ⓐ TRUE   Ⓑ FALSE   Ⓒ CANNOT SAY

2 The issue of free plastic carrier bags has received much more coverage than the issue of supermarket refrigeration.

Ⓐ TRUE   Ⓑ FALSE   Ⓒ CANNOT SAY

3 Supermarket fridges are a much greater threat to the environment than plastic bags.

Ⓐ TRUE   Ⓑ FALSE   Ⓒ CANNOT SAY

4 Carbon dioxide and ammonia do not harm the ozone layer.

Ⓐ TRUE   Ⓑ FALSE   Ⓒ CANNOT SAY

5 HFC gases are not environmentally damaging like CFC gases.

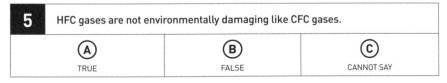

Ⓐ TRUE   Ⓑ FALSE   Ⓒ CANNOT SAY

SUPERMARKET FREEZERS COME IN FROM THE COLD

1 2 Most leading supermarkets have reacted to the high-profile campaign to minimise the use of plastic carrier bags by selling re-useable bags, no longer offering customers free plastic bags or charging for them. Environmentalists are critical of these actions, pointing out that by far **3 the biggest source of environmental threat posed by supermarkets is not plastic bags but refrigeration.**

A recent study showed that 30% of the environmentally damaging chemicals emitted by supermarkets are due to leakage from fridges and freezers. The gases commonly used in refrigeration units as a coolant are called **5 HFCs (hydrofluorocarbons) and while they do not damage the ozone layer like the old fashioned CFC gases they do contribute to global warming.**

Fridges and freezers leak HFC gases over time. The total leakage from supermarkets is equivalent to one billion car journeys to a supermarket or the production of 5.6 billion plastic bags.

2 Until now this issue has received far less attention than the less environmentally damaging issue of free plastic bags. But now the supermarket chain SuperStoreUK has announced plans to introduce new refrigeration technology into all its stores over the next five years. These new fridges and freezers use **4 carbon dioxide and ammonia instead of HFCs and are therefore less harmful to the environment.**

1 Supermarkets accept the arguments of the campaign to minimise the use of free plastic carrier bags.

Correct answer is C: Cannot say – supermarkets have introduced measures to reduce the use of free plastic bags (see the first line of the passage) but there is no information that this action was based on an agreement with the arguments of the campaign. The supermarkets could simply be reacting to public opinion. It would be wrong to base your answer on an assumption either way.

2 The issue of free plastic carrier bags has received much more coverage than the issue of supermarket refrigeration.

Correct answer is A: True – you can see that the statement is true in the highlighted text in the first line of the final paragraph of the verbal information – the plastic bags issue has received more attention.

3 Supermarket fridges are a much greater threat to the environment than plastic bags.

Correct answer is A: True – you can see that the statement is true in the highlighted text in the last line of the first paragraph of the verbal information – HFC gases from supermarket refrigeration are more environmentally damaging than plastic bags.

4 Carbon dioxide and ammonia do not harm the ozone layer.

Correct answer is C: Cannot say – the highlighted text in the final paragraph explains that carbon dioxide and ammonia are therefore less harmful to the environment but does not state whether or not these gases harm the ozone layer.

5 HFC gases are not environmentally damaging like CFC gases.

Correct answer is B: False – the last two lines of the second paragraph state that HFCs do not damage the ozone layer like CFCs, but they are still environmentally damaging since they contribute to global warming.

Score of 5	Score of 4	Score of 3	Score of 2	Score of 1
Great performance	Good performance	Average performance	Below average performance	Poor performance

SUPERMARKET FREEZERS COME IN FROM THE COLD

Most leading supermarkets have reacted to the high-profile campaign to minimise the use of plastic carrier bags by selling re-useable bags, no longer offering customers free plastic bags or charging for them. Environmentalists are critical of these actions, pointing out that by far the biggest source of environmental threat posed by supermarkets is not plastic bags but refrigeration.

A recent study showed that 30% of the environmentally damaging chemicals emitted by supermarkets are due to leakage from fridges and freezers. The gases commonly used in refrigeration units as a coolant are called HFCs (hydrofluorocarbons) and while they do not damage the ozone layer like the old fashioned CFC gases they do contribute to global warming.

Fridges and freezers leak HFC gases over time. The total leakage from supermarkets is equivalent to one billion car journeys to a supermarket or the production of 5.6 billion plastic bags.

Until now this issue has received far less attention that the less environmentally damaging issue of free plastic bags. But now the supermarket chain SuperStoreUK has announced plans to introduce new refrigeration technology into all its stores over the next five years. These new fridges and freezers use carbon dioxide and ammonia instead of HFCs and are therefore less harmful to the environment.

A	B	C
TRUE	**FALSE**	**CANNOT SAY**
Fill in **A** if the statement is **True** from the information given.	Fill in **B** if the statement is **False** from the information given.	Fill in **C** if you **Cannot say** for certain from the information given whether the statement is true or false.

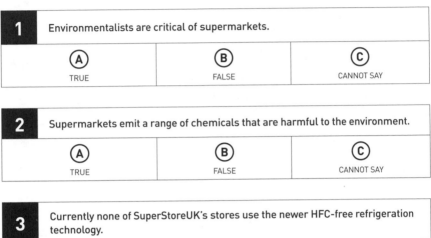

1   Environmentalists are critical of supermarkets.

Ⓐ	Ⓑ	Ⓒ
TRUE	FALSE	CANNOT SAY

2   Supermarkets emit a range of chemicals that are harmful to the environment.

Ⓐ	Ⓑ	Ⓒ
TRUE	FALSE	CANNOT SAY

3   Currently none of SuperStoreUK's stores use the newer HFC-free refrigeration technology.

Ⓐ	Ⓑ	Ⓒ
TRUE	FALSE	CANNOT SAY

4   Most supermarkets no longer have non-reusable plastic bags for their customers.

Ⓐ	Ⓑ	Ⓒ
TRUE	FALSE	CANNOT SAY

5   Only old or damaged fridges and freezers leak HFC gases.

Ⓐ	Ⓑ	Ⓒ
TRUE	FALSE	CANNOT SAY

SUPERMARKET FREEZERS COME IN FROM THE COLD

4 Most leading supermarkets have reacted to the high-profile campaign to minimise the use of plastic carrier bags by selling re-useable bags, no longer offering customers free plastic bags or charging for them. **1** Environmentalists are critical of these actions, pointing out that by far the biggest source of environmental threat posed by supermarkets is not plastic bags but refrigeration.

2 A recent study showed that 30% of the environmentally damaging chemicals emitted by supermarkets are due to leakage from fridges and freezers. The gases commonly used in refrigeration units as a coolant are called HFCs (hydrofluorocarbons) and while they do not damage the ozone layer like the old fashioned CFC gases they do contribute to global warming.

5 Fridges and freezers leak HFC gases over time. The total leakage from supermarkets is equivalent to one billion car journeys to a supermarket or the production of 5.6 billion plastic bags.

Until now this issue has received far less attention that the less environmentally damaging issue of free plastic bags. But now the supermarket chain **3** SuperStoreUK has announced plans to introduce new refrigeration technology into all its stores over the next five years. These new fridges and freezers use carbon dioxide and ammonia instead of HFCs and are therefore less harmful to the environment.

1 Environmentalists are critical of supermarkets.

Correct answer is C: Cannot say – the highlighted text in the first paragraph states that environmentalists are critical of the actions taken to reduce plastic bag usage. The passage does not state explicitly that environmentalists are critical of supermarkets themselves, only the actions described. It would be wrong to answer true or false on the basis of the information given.

2 Supermarkets emit a range of chemicals that are harmful to the environment.

Correct answer is A: True – you can see that the statement is true in the highlighted text in the first line of the second paragraph of the verbal information – HFC gases account for 30% of the environmentally damaging chemicals emitted by supermarkets. The remaining 70% must be made up of chemicals that are not HFCs; the statement is therefore true because supermarkets emit chemicals other than HFCs.

3 Currently none of SuperStoreUK's stores use the newer HFC-free refrigeration technology.

Correct answer is C: Cannot say – the highlighted text in the final paragraph states that SuperStoreUK will introduce the new fridges and freezers into all of its stores in the next five years. We can therefore infer that some of the stores may already have the new technology – but we cannot say for certain that none of the stores currently use it. The answer is therefore Cannot say.

4 Most supermarkets no longer have non-reusable plastic bags for their customers.

Correct answer is B: False – the first line of the passage states that most supermarkets either no longer offer customers free plastic bags or charge for them, which is not the same as no longer having them available for customers.

5 Only old or damaged fridges and freezers leak HFC gases.

Correct answer is B: False – the first line of the third paragraph states that fridges and freezers leak HFC gases over time, not just when old or damaged. The correct answer is therefore false.

How did you do?

Score of 5	Score of 4	Score of 3	Score of 2	Score of 1
Great performance	Good performance	Average performance	Below average performance	Poor performance

NERO: THE NATIONAL ENVIRONMENTAL RESEARCH ORGANISATION

A **Balanced Scorecard** is used by NERO to help monitor the performance of the organisation. The metrics that our balanced scorecard contains ensure that we translate our strategy into actions. The Balanced Scorecard measures our progression towards achieving our vision of success.

The underlying rationale for adopting a Balanced Scorecard is that organisations cannot directly influence financial outcomes, as these are 'lag' measures, and that the use of financial measures alone to inform strategic control of a business is unwise. We therefore also measure those areas where direct management intervention is possible. In so doing, the Balanced Scorecard helps us achieve a 'balance' in the selection of performance measures.

Our Balanced Scorecard contains four measures, which ensure that our actions are focused on our customers, our processes and our people as well as more traditional financial outcomes.

1. The **financial** measure examines whether our implementation and execution of our vision and values are contributing to our bottom line. It represents our long-term strategic objectives and incorporates the tangible outcomes of the strategy in traditional financial terms. Our current financial strategy is to reduce our running costs and improve our forecasting accuracy.
2. The **client** measure describes how we intend to generate more sales to the most desired (i.e. the most profitable) customer groups. Our current client strategy is to grow our key government client and gain two new private sector clients.
3. The **internal business process** measure is concerned with the activities and key processes required for us to excel at providing the value expected by the customers both productively and efficiently.
4. The **learning and growth** measure is the foundation of our strategy and it focuses on the internal skills and capabilities that are required. Our current learning and growth strategy is to strengthen our business planning capability and build our leadership capabilities.

A	B	C
TRUE	**FALSE**	**CANNOT SAY**
Fill in **A** if the statement is **True** from the information given.	Fill in **B** if the statement is **False** from the information given.	Fill in **C** if you **Cannot say** for certain from the information given whether the statement is true or false.

---

1 The Balanced Scorecard used by NERO tracks the performance of the organisation.

(A)	(B)	(C)
TRUE	FALSE	CANNOT SAY

---

2 Financial measures are a poor indicator of business performance.

(A)	(B)	(C)
TRUE	FALSE	CANNOT SAY

---

3 The Balanced Scorecard measures areas that the management of an organisation can influence.

(A)	(B)	(C)
TRUE	FALSE	CANNOT SAY

---

4 Financial indicators can take some time to influence.

(A)	(B)	(C)
TRUE	FALSE	CANNOT SAY

---

5 Choices about strategy should be based solely on financial performance indicators.

(A)	(B)	(C)
TRUE	FALSE	CANNOT SAY

NERO: THE NATIONAL ENVIRONMENTAL RESEARCH ORGANISATION

A **1** **Balanced Scorecard is used by NERO to help monitor the performance of the organisation**. The metrics that our Balanced Scorecard contains ensure that we translate our strategy into actions. The Balanced Scorecard measures our progression towards achieving our vision of success.

The underlying rationale for adopting a Balanced Scorecard is that organisations cannot directly **4** **influence financial outcomes, as these are 'lag' measures,** and that **2** **5** **the use of financial measures alone to inform strategic control of a business is unwise**. We therefore also **3** **measure those areas where direct management intervention is possible.** In so doing, the Balanced Scorecard helps us achieve a 'balance' in the selection of performance measures.

Our Balanced Scorecard contains four measures, which ensure that our actions are focused on our customers, our processes and our people as well as more traditional financial outcomes.

1. The **financial** measure examines whether our implementation and execution of our vision and values are contributing to our bottom line. It represents our long-term strategic objectives and incorporates the tangible outcomes of the strategy in traditional financial terms. Our current financial strategy is to reduce our running costs and improve our forecasting accuracy.
2. The **client** measure describes how we intend to generate more sales to the most desired (i.e. the most profitable) customer groups. Our current client strategy is to grow our key government client and gain two new private sector clients.
3. The **internal business process** measure is concerned with the activities and key processes required for us to excel at providing the value expected by the customers both productively and efficiently.
4. The **learning and growth** measure is the foundation of our strategy and it focuses on the internal skills and capabilities that are required. Our current learning and growth strategy is to strengthen our business planning capability and build our leadership capabilities.

| **1** | The Balanced Scorecard used by NERO tracks the performance of the organisation. |

Correct answer is A: True – you can see that the statement is true in the highlighted text in the first line of the first paragraph of the verbal information – NERO uses its Balanced Scorecard to help monitor its performance.

| **2** | Financial measures are a poor indicator of business performance. |

Correct answer is C: Cannot say – the highlighted text in the second paragraph describes the use of financial measures alone to inform strategic control of a business as 'unwise'. It would be wrong to assume from this information that financial measures are poor indicators; we can only infer that they should not be used in isolation from other measures of performance. Conversely we cannot assume that financial indictors are good measures either. The answer is therefore Cannot say.

| **3** | The Balanced Scorecard measures areas that the management of an organisation can influence. |

Correct answer is A: True – you can see that the statement is true in the highlighted text in the fifth line of the second paragraph of the verbal information – NERO measures areas where direct management intervention is possible and uses the Balanced Scorecard to do this.

| **4** | Financial indicators can take some time to influence. |

Correct answer is A: True – you can see that the statement is true in the highlighted text in the second line of the second paragraph of the verbal information – financial outcomes are described as 'lag' measures (in other words there is a delay, or lag, before they show the results of any actions). The correct answer is true because there can be some time before financial measures change as a result of any actions taken to influence them.

| **5** | Choices about strategy should be based solely on financial performance indicators. |

Correct answer is B: False – the third line of the second paragraph states that the use of financial measures alone to inform strategic control of a business is unwise. The correct answer is therefore False, because the information states that it is unwise to use financial indicators on their own.

How did you do?

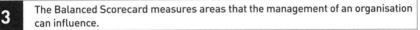

Score of 5	Score of 4	Score of 3	Score of 2	Score of 1
Great performance	Good performance	Average performance	Below average performance	Poor performance

NERO: THE NATIONAL ENVIRONMENTAL RESEARCH ORGANISATION

A **Balanced Scorecard** is used by NERO to help monitor the performance of the organisation. The metrics that our Balanced Scorecard contains ensure that we translate our strategy into actions. The Balanced Scorecard measures our progression towards achieving our vision of success.

The underlying rationale for adopting a Balanced Scorecard is that organisations cannot directly influence financial outcomes, as these are 'lag' measures, and that the use of financial measures alone to inform strategic control of a business is unwise. We therefore also measure those areas where direct management intervention is possible. In so doing, the Balanced Scorecard helps us achieve a 'balance' in the selection of performance measures.

Our Balanced Scorecard contains four measures, which ensure that our actions are focused on our customers, our processes and our people as well as more traditional financial outcomes.

1. The **financial** measure examines whether our implementation and execution of our vision and values are contributing to our bottom line. It represents our long-term strategic objectives and incorporates the tangible outcomes of the strategy in traditional financial terms. Our current financial strategy is to reduce our running costs and improve our forecasting accuracy.
2. The **client** measure describes how we intend to generate more sales to the most desired (i.e. the most profitable) customer groups. Our current client strategy is to grow our key government client and gain two new private sector clients.
3. The **internal business process** measure is concerned with the activities and key processes required for us to excel at providing the value expected by the customers both productively and efficiently.
4. The **learning and growth** measure is the foundation of our strategy and it focuses on the internal skills and capabilities that are required. Our current learning and growth strategy is to strengthen our business planning capability and build our leadership capabilities.

A	B	C
TRUE	**FALSE**	**CANNOT SAY**
Fill in **A** if the statement is **True** from the information given.	Fill in **B** if the statement is **False** from the information given.	Fill in **C** if you **Cannot say** for certain from the information given whether the statement is true or false.

1 Each of the performance measures in the Balanced Scorecard is equally weighted.

Ⓐ TRUE   Ⓑ FALSE   Ⓒ CANNOT SAY

2 NERO's long-term strategy is not concerned with the financial performance of the organisation.

Ⓐ TRUE   Ⓑ FALSE   Ⓒ CANNOT SAY

3 The value of customers is judged purely in terms of their contribution to the bottom-line of the business.

Ⓐ TRUE   Ⓑ FALSE   Ⓒ CANNOT SAY

4 NERO's customers have high expectations of the organisation and its work.

Ⓐ TRUE   Ⓑ FALSE   Ⓒ CANNOT SAY

5 NERO has some capabilities that are in need of improvement.

Ⓐ TRUE   Ⓑ FALSE   Ⓒ CANNOT SAY

NERO: THE NATIONAL ENVIRONMENTAL RESEARCH ORGANISATION

A **Balanced Scorecard** is used by NERO to help monitor the performance of the organisation. The metrics that our Balanced Scorecard contains ensure that we translate our strategy into actions. The Balanced Scorecard measures our progression towards achieving our vision of success.

The underlying rationale for adopting a Balanced Scorecard is that organisations cannot directly influence financial outcomes, as these are 'lag' measures, and that the use of financial measures alone to inform strategic control of a business is unwise. We therefore also measure those areas where direct management intervention is possible. In so doing, **1 the Balanced Scorecard helps us achieve a 'balance' in the selection of performance measures**.

Our Balanced Scorecard contains four measures, which ensure that our actions are focused on our customers, our processes and our people as well as more traditional financial outcomes.

1. The **financial** measure examines whether our implementation and execution of our vision and values are contributing to our bottom line. **2 It represents our long-term strategic objectives and incorporates the tangible outcomes of the strategy in traditional financial terms.** Our current financial strategy is to reduce our running costs and improve our forecasting accuracy.

2. The **client measure** describes how we intend to generate more sales to **3 the most desired (i.e. the most profitable) customer groups**. Our current client strategy is to grow our key government client and gain two new private sector clients.

3. The **internal business process** measure is concerned with the activities and key processes required for us to excel at providing **4 the value expected by the customers** both productively and efficiently.

4. The **learning and growth** measure is the foundation of our strategy and it focuses on the internal skills and capabilities that are required. Our current learning and growth strategy is **5 to strengthen our business planning capability and build our leadership capabilities**.

1 Each of the performance measures in the Balanced Scorecard is equally weighted.

Correct answer is C: Cannot say – the highlighted text at the end of the second paragraph states that the Balanced Scorecard helps NERO to achieve a 'balance' in the selection of performance measures. The information does not specify whether or not the weighting is equal among the measures – only that they achieve a balance when put together. The answer is therefore Cannot say.

2 NERO's long-term strategy is not concerned with the financial performance of the organisation.

Correct answer is B: False – the description of the financial measure states that it represents their long-term strategic objectives and incorporates the tangible outcomes of the strategy in traditional financial terms. The long-term strategy of the organisation therefore does include a focus on financial performance; the statement is therefore false.

3 The value of customers is judged purely in terms of their contribution to the bottom-line of the business.

Correct answer is C: Cannot say – the highlighted text in the description of the client measure states that the most desired customer groups are the most profitable. We cannot assume that the profitability of customers is the only way in which their value is judged by the business. The answer is therefore Cannot say.

4 NERO's customers have high expectations of the organisation and its work.

Correct answer is C: Cannot say – the highlighted text in the description of the internal processes measure states that NERO's customers do expect value from the organisation but the passage does not state explicitly that customers' expectations of the value delivered by NERO are high or low. We therefore cannot say for certain that this statement is true or false.

5 NERO has some capabilities that are in need of improvement.

Correct answer is A: True – you can see that the statement is true in the highlighted text in the final paragraph of the passage. NERO wants to strengthen its business planning capability and leadership capabilities. The statement is therefore true because NERO does need to make improvements in some areas of skill and capability.

How did you do?

Score of 5	Score of 4	Score of 3	Score of 2	Score of 1
Great performance	Good performance	Average performance	Below average performance	Poor performance

THE DRUGS DON'T WORK

Pharmaceutical research and development is expensive and time-consuming, costing by latest estimates nearly one billion US dollars for each new chemical entity and taking 10 to 15 years on average from discovery to market authorisation. In recent years, despite increasing expenditure on pharmaceutical innovation, the number of new medicines being authorised is disappointingly low.

The factors that can act as barriers to pharmaceutical innovation are complex interrelations between the scientific, clinical, regulatory and financial considerations. Although different stakeholders have divergent points of view with regard to what the barriers are, and how to overcome them, recently a series of documents by different stakeholders in drug development have appeared discussing barriers to pharmaceutical innovation. The congruence of the factors identified and the policy conclusions among these documents are encouraging. Barriers to innovation, in broad outline, may include:

▶ Inadequate understanding of basic science for certain diseases and the identification of targets amenable to manipulation.
▶ Regulatory authority 'rituals' with regard to preclinical and clinical testing procedures that may, or may not, have basis in empirical evidence.
▶ Differences in perception of risk among different stakeholders.
▶ Uncertainty about the timing and level of reimbursement decisions leading to uncertainty among stakeholders.
▶ General business uncertainties in drug development.
▶ Potential increases in the cost of doing business due to intellectual property concerns.

The EU Commission has recently called, within its sixth Framework Work Program for Thematic Priority 1 (life sciences, genomics and biotechnology), for research proposals that include new approaches for accelerated development of new, safe and more effective medicines.

As part of this call for proposals, the EU should create and support a broad research agenda so that every requirement within the drug development process is questioned for its relevance, costing, and predictive value.

A	B	C
TRUE	**FALSE**	**CANNOT SAY**
Fill in **A** if the statement is **True** from the information given.	Fill in **B** if the statement is **False** from the information given.	Fill in **C** if you **Cannot say** for certain from the information given whether the statement is true or false.

---

1 Most medicines that are developed are authorised for sale.

(A)	(B)	(C)
TRUE	FALSE	CANNOT SAY

---

2 Consensus among stakeholders in drug development about barriers to innovation is unlikely to ever be achieved.

(A)	(B)	(C)
TRUE	FALSE	CANNOT SAY

---

3 It is difficult to select measures in drug studies that the developers can influence.

(A)	(B)	(C)
TRUE	FALSE	CANNOT SAY

---

4 The EU has a great deal of influence over the regulatory requirements for drug development.

(A)	(B)	(C)
TRUE	FALSE	CANNOT SAY

---

5 Some drug development stakeholders have a more relaxed attitude towards risk than others.

(A)	(B)	(C)
TRUE	FALSE	CANNOT SAY

THE DRUGS DON'T WORK

Pharmaceutical research and development is expensive and time-consuming, costing by latest estimates nearly one billion US dollars for each new chemical entity and taking 10 to 15 years on average from discovery to market authorisation. In recent years, despite increasing expenditure on pharmaceutical innovation, **1** **the number of new medicines being authorised is disappointingly low**.

The factors that can act as barriers to pharmaceutical innovation are complex interrelations between the scientific, clinical, regulatory and financial considerations. Although different stakeholders have divergent points of view with regard to what the barriers are, and how to overcome them, recently, **2** **a series of documents by different stakeholders in drug development have appeared discussing barriers to pharmaceutical innovation. The congruence of the factors identified and the policy conclusions among these documents are encouraging**. Barriers to innovation, in broad outline, may include:

- Inadequate understanding of basic science for certain diseases and **3** **the identification of targets amenable to manipulation**.
- Regulatory authority 'rituals' with regard to preclinical and clinical testing procedures that may, or may not, have basis in empirical evidence.
- **5** **Differences in perception of risk among different stakeholders**
- Uncertainty about the timing and level of reimbursement decisions leading to uncertainty among stakeholders.
- General business uncertainties in drug development
- Potential increases in the cost of doing business due to intellectual property concerns.

The EU Commission has recently called, within its sixth Framework Work Program for Thematic Priority 1 (life sciences, genomics and biotechnology), for research proposals that include new approaches for accelerated development of new, safe and more effective medicines.

As part of this call for proposals, **4** **the EU should create and support a broad research agenda so that every requirement within the drug development process is questioned** for its relevance, costing, and predictive value.

| **1** | Most medicines that are developed are authorised for sale. |

Correct answer is B: False – the final clause of the first paragraph states that the number of new medicines being authorised is disappointingly low. We can therefore infer that the statement is false because only a small number of medicines become authorised, not the majority.

| **2** | Consensus among stakeholders in drug development about barriers to innovation is unlikely to ever be achieved. |

Correct answer is B: False – the highlighted text in the second paragraph describes how a number of stakeholders have worked together to produce documents describing the main barriers to innovation and what can be done about it. The information states that there is an encouraging level of congruence, or agreement, between these documents, from which we can infer that some consensus between the stakeholders already exists. It is therefore false to say that consensus is unlikely to be achieved. The correct answer is False.

| **3** | It is difficult to select measures in drug studies that the developers can influence. |

Correct answer is A: True – the first bullet point describing the barriers to innovation in drug development states that it is hard to identify targets that are amenable to manipulation. In other words, a difficulty within drug studies is finding measures of success (targets) that the developers of the drug can try to achieve through making changes to their new drugs – they are not amenable to manipulation. The statement is therefore true.

| **4** | The EU has a great deal of influence over the regulatory requirements for drug development. |

Correct answer is C: Cannot say – the highlighted text in the final paragraph states that the EU should create and support a broad research agenda so that every requirement within the drug development process is questioned. This suggests a degree of influence over the regulatory requirements but we cannot infer with certainty that the EU has a great deal of influence. The answer is therefore Cannot say.

| **5** | Some drug development stakeholders have a more relaxed attitude towards risk than others. |

Correct answer is A: True – the third bullet point describing the barriers to innovation in drug development states that the drug developers vary in their levels of perception of risk. We can infer that some must have a higher tolerance of risk than others and would therefore be more relaxed about risk. The statement is therefore true.

How did you do?

Score of 5	Score of 4	Score of 3	Score of 2	Score of 1
Great performance	Good performance	Average performance	Below average performance	Poor performance

A CHANGE OF PACE FOR THE FINAL PRACTICE TEST

Well done for working through the first nine verbal critical-reasoning tests. Did you notice any change in the difficulty of the questions as you progressed? You may have been aware of a shift in your verbal ability as you worked through all the questions.

The next verbal critical-reasoning test is the tenth and final set of practice questions and is a little different from the previous nine practice tests. The test uses the usual format applied by modern occupational tests of verbal ability – it has a passage of verbal information followed by some multiple-choice questions. This time though the test uses a range of multiple-choice formats.

We've varied the format so that you can see that while the formats may vary, the approach you have developed over the course of your work so far need not. The practice and skills you have developed will transfer seamlessly to the other formats.

INSTRUCTIONS FOR PRACTICE TEST 10

The instructions for this test are identical to the previous practice tests. You should read the verbal information and then evaluate each of the questions about the text. For each question you must pick the answer you think is correct from the options given. You must base your answers on the information given.

This test contains six questions and you should allow yourself eight minutes to complete it.

CBT: THE TALKING CURE FOR MODERN LIFE

Over the last 30 years, the field of Cognitive Behavioural Psychology has yielded a range of highly effective methods for enabling people to change their thoughts and feelings, and, consequently, to improve their quality of life.

Cognitive Behavioural Therapy (CBT) is based on the idea that we are what we think. It is not life's events that make us feel good or bad; it is the way we interpret these events. These interpretations are based on our attitudes and beliefs. Once we understand that our interpretations of events are the key, we can look for new and positive interpretations.

The methods that enable people to change, help people to focus on their beliefs and attitudes. These methods have been used in many ways. They have been used as fast and effective therapies for the treatment of emotional illnesses, such as anxiety and depression. They have been used in 'positive attitude training' for people suffering from emotional problems. They have been used to improve people's performance and motivation in the workplace, and by sports psychologists to enable their clients to fulfil their potential.

Most, perhaps all, people could benefit from understanding and developing their personal attitudes and beliefs. For some people this would help them to re-interpret (or 'reframe') events that have caused them distress, such as a relationship breakdown, or losing a job. For others, benefit would arise from focusing on more general self-beliefs or attitudes to life.

In order to understand and develop their attitudes and beliefs, most people need a counsellor or therapist. Clients attend a series of sessions with their therapist, who will help them to explore and develop their attitudes and beliefs, using the methods and techniques of CBT.

1 People have solved their emotional problems by using techniques from cognitive behavioural therapy.

A. The statement is **True** from the information given.
B. The statement is **False** from the information given.
C. You **Cannot say** for certain from the information given whether the statement is true or false.

2 Which of these statements most accurately reflects the principles of Cognitive Behavioural Therapy?

A. Our interpretations of events are driven by our feelings.
B. Some events are good and some are bad.
C. Our feelings are the result of our interpretations of events.
D. Our attitudes are based on our feelings.

3 Which of these statements most accurately reflects the methods of Cognitive Behavioural Therapy?

A. There is only one way to interpret the events we experience.
B. We must change our beliefs in order to change our interpretations of events.
C. People must improve the quality of their life to be happier.
D. Changing our interpretations of events will change our values and attitudes.

4 Sports psychologists use CBT to help clients with depression.

A. The statement is **True** from the information given.
B. The statement is **False** from the information given.
C. You **Cannot say** for certain from the information given whether the statement is true or false.

5 Which of these words would best replace 'explore' in this statement without changing the meaning of the passage? *Clients attend a series of sessions with their therapist, who will help them to **explore** and develop their attitudes and beliefs.*

A. Research
B. Learn
C. Study
D. Understand

6 Which of these statements most accurately reflects the theory of Cognitive Behavioural Therapy?

A. People can learn to reframe negative experiences.
B. Only a minority of people would benefit from working on their attitudes and beliefs.
C. CBT is only appropriate for people with problems and issues.
D. CBT only requires a single session with a therapist.

CBT: THE TALKING CURE FOR MODERN LIFE

Over the last 30 years, the field of Cognitive Behavioural Psychology has yielded a range of **1** **highly effective methods for enabling people to change their thoughts and feelings, and, consequently, to improve their quality of life.**

Cognitive Behavioural Therapy (CBT) is based on the idea that we are what we think. **2** **It is not life's events that make us feel good or bad; it is the way we interpret these events.** **3** **These interpretations are based on our attitudes and beliefs.** Once we understand that our interpretations of events are the key, we can look for new and positive interpretations.

The methods that enable people to change, help people to focus on their beliefs and attitudes. These methods have been used in many ways. **1** **They have been used as fast and effective therapies for the treatment of emotional illnesses, such as anxiety and depression.** They have been used in 'positive attitude training' for people suffering from emotional problems. They have been used to improve people's performance and motivation in the workplace, and by **4** **sports psychologists to enable their clients to fulfil their potential**.

Most, perhaps all, people could benefit from understanding and developing their personal attitudes and beliefs. **6** **For some people this would help them to re-interpret (or 'reframe') events that have caused them distress**, such as a relationship breakdown, or losing a job. For others, benefit would arise from focusing on more general self-beliefs or attitudes to life.

In order to understand and develop their attitudes and beliefs, most people need a counsellor or therapist. Clients attend a series of sessions with their therapist, who will help them to explore and develop their attitudes and beliefs, using the methods and techniques of CBT.

| 1 | People have solved their emotional problems by using techniques from cognitive behavioural therapy. |

Correct answer is A: True – highlighted text in the first and third paragraphs describes how CBT uses effective methods for improving the quality of people's lives and tackling emotional problems. The statement is therefore true.

| 2 | Which of these statements most accurately reflects the principles of Cognitive Behavioural Therapy? |

The correct answer is: C Our feelings are the result of our interpretations of events. The highlighted text starting in the second line of the second paragraph describes how our feelings are determined by the way we interpret events as good or bad. None of the other statements in this question are supported by the information in the passage.

| 3 | Which of these statements most accurately reflects the methods of Cognitive Behavioural Therapy? |

The correct answer is: B We must change our beliefs in order to change our interpretations of events. The third and fourth lines of the second paragraph describe how our interpretations of events are driven by our attitudes, beliefs and values. None of the other statements in this question are supported by the information in the passage.

| 4 | Sports Psychologists use CBT to help clients with depression. |

Correct answer is C: Cannot say – The highlighted text in the third paragraph states that sport psychologists use CBT to help their clients fulfil their potential and this could include clients with depression. We must not infer from the earlier part of the paragraph about positive attitude training that sports psychologists do not work with emotional problems like depression using CBT. We cannot say for certain whether sports psychologists help their clients with depression or not.

| 5 | Which of these words would best replace 'explore' in this statement without changing the meaning of the passage? *Clients attend a series of sessions with their therapist, who will help them to **explore** and develop their attitudes and beliefs* |

Correct answer is D: Understand. While the other words are all alternative meanings for the word 'explore', only the word 'understand' accurately captures the meaning of this part of the passage, which describes how clients are helped by their therapist to talk about, discover and understand their attitudes through exploration in order to develop alternatives.

| 6 | Which of these statements most accurately reflects the theory of Cognitive Behavioural Therapy? |

Correct answer is A: People can learn to re-frame negative experiences. The highlighted text in the fourth paragraph states that people can learn to re-frame distressing events. None of the other statements in this question are supported by the information in the passage.

How did you do?

Score of 6	Score of 5	Score of 3–4	Score of 2	Score of 1
Great performance	Good performance	Average performance	Below average performance	Poor performance

TOTAL SCORES: RATE YOUR PERFORMANCE

These practice tests are too short individually to make an accurate measurement of your verbal ability, but if you put your results together we can provide a clearer view. Add the scores from each of the 10 practice tests together and compare your total score with the table below to gauge your performance.

Total score	What it means	Advice for further development
50+	Excellent performance	It looks like you're pretty much there in terms of developing your personal best score. Don't rest on your laurels though. Make sure that you take the time to work through the remaining sections of this book; they contain information that will help you maintain this level of performance. Also, remember to keep exercising your raw verbal ability through reading, solving puzzles and taking part in discussions. This way you can keep your ability at its strongest up until your next test.
40–49	Good performance	This level of performance should see you through most verbal tests, but if you feel that it does not reflect your potential personal best score then you might want to do some more practice. Review the advice in Chapter 2 about test strategies and practising advice and then have another go at the practice questions.
30–39	Average performance	Verbal critical reasoning tests are the hardest type of verbal assessment you are likely to take, so an average score is still a positive result. However, you could benefit from doing some more work to practise and pass verbal tests at this level more effortlessly. Review the advice in

Total score	What it means	Advice for further development
		Chapter 2 about test strategies and practice advice. You can also review your wrong answers to the practice questions to try and identify any trends in where you go wrong. It might be that the tricky 'cannot say' answers give you the most trouble. Whatever the case, spend some time reviewing where you went wrong and then attempt the practice questions again.
20–29	Below average performance	These are high-level tests so you might want to polish your verbal ability by correcting any shortfalls in your verbal reasoning abilities by revisiting your work in Chapter 4. Once you are happy that your performance at those mid-level tests reflects your true potential you should return to these verbal critical-reasoning tests. To begin with do not apply the time-limits when you attempt these high-level tests – and see if that makes a difference. If time is a factor then you should identify which areas of your test-taking strategy might be letting you down. Spend some time developing and exercising your raw verbal ability through reading, solving puzzles and taking part in discussions alongside further practice from this book.
0–19	Low performance	

Remember that these 10 practice tests are pitched at the highest level you are likely to encounter at work. If your personal best is not within the top range of the results then it might simply be the case that your strengths lie elsewhere – perhaps within another ability like your numerical reasoning. You can offset a deficit within one area of your performance by focusing on your strengths. If you are going to complete a verbal test it is likely that you will be asked to complete a different test alongside it. You can maximise your overall performance by developing all of the abilities you are tested on. Consider working through other books in the *Practice & Pass* series to help you build on all your strengths.

CHAPTER 6
ONLINE VERBAL TESTING

The traditional format for verbal ability testing is using paper and pencil materials and a test administration session held under supervised conditions, typically with groups of other people. Over the course of the last 10 years this has changed, with employers using the internet to deliver tests to their candidates. Today, if you are asked to take a test for an employer, it is very likely that you will complete it online. This change in testing format has implications for your personal best score, which are explored in this chapter.

HOW IT WORKS

Online testing is most commonly used by large employers within high-volume recruitment processes. The greater the number of people who apply for a vacancy, the greater the likelihood that the employer will adopt online testing instead of paper and pencil testing. However, employers also use online testing for a range of purposes unconnected with recruitment. Many of our clients ask their training delegates to complete an online test before they attend a leadership development programme, therefore saving time during the course itself which would otherwise have been taken up with a testing session. This saved time can be devoted to exploring the results of the test.

There are two common alternative approaches to online testing.

▶ **Supervised online testing.** This approach is not all that different from traditional paper and pencil testing. To complete the verbal test you attend the employer's testing centre (their offices or another location) and complete the test on a computer in the presence of a test administrator, who oversees the testing session. The only difference is that you are completing the test on a computer rather than with paper and pencil materials.

If you are asked to complete an online test under supervision then there is little difference with traditional testing in terms of the approach you should take to achieving your personal best scores.

INSIDER INFO

FREE ONLINE TESTS

A quick internet search for free online verbal tests will yield millions of results – but take care, because the vast majority will be of questionable quality compared to the tests used by employers to select people for recruitment and development.

Reputable online ability tests are built to high standards of accuracy and have been subjected to research to ensure that they are fit for purpose. Test publishers in the UK submit their tests for review by the British Psychological Society to enable test-users to make informed decisions about which tests to use based on the technical qualities of the test.

If you are looking online for a practice verbal test you are encouraged to restrict your search to UK-based test publishers. This way you can feel confident that any practice questions you complete are representative of the format, style and quality of real psychometric tests of ability.

You can find a list of online practice tests in Chapter 9.

▶ **Unsupervised remote online testing.** This approach is the most favoured by employers because it benefits them in terms of time and cost. Instead of inviting candidates to complete the test under supervision, the test administrator sends candidates a link and password for the online verbal test. Candidates complete the online test at a time and location of their choosing. This approach removes the requirement for the employer to provide a testing location or people to oversee the test session.

If you are asked to complete an online verbal test remotely and unsupervised you may need to adapt your approach in order to maintain the level of performance you'd expect to achieve in a traditional testing session. The first step is to understand the differences between traditional testing and unsupervised online testing.

WHAT ARE THE DIFFERENCES?

The obvious difference between an online test and a traditional paper and pencil test is the format. You complete the test using a computer connected to the internet, which displays the test instructions, the verbal information and the verbal questions. You give your answers on-screen rather than on a separate answer sheet.

The unsupervised element of online verbal testing means that you will take the test alone, at a time and place of your choosing, with no test administrator watching you. For many people this is a relief from the stressful environment of the traditional test session.

You are required to provide the testing materials in the sense that you need to find an internet-connected computer to complete the test. This is an aspect of the cost of testing that the employer is passing on to you. For many people this presents no problem since they have access to a computer at home or work; but it can cause difficulties for those who are unconnected.

While you are expected to provide the testing materials the remote nature of the online verbal test does offer you savings in terms of travel costs to the employer's place of business to be tested. Our earliest clients to adopt online testing did so because previously they needed to fly candidates into their UK office from all over Europe and Asia to be tested. Remote testing had clear benefits for the employer and the candidates.

Your results are calculated by the online testing system rather than the test administrator, who traditionally would have to calculate results by hand. The benefit for you as the test-taker is the removal of any possible scoring error that might adversely affect your score.

When the employer is using the online test for recruitment they will often use your verbal test results, alongside any other information you have provided such as a CV or application form, to make a pre-selection decision. This means the employer sifts out any applicants whose verbal test score and supporting information indicate low suitability for the job. Only candidates with the right level of ability combined with the right experience will be invited to interview. Many candidates worry about this high-stakes nature of the online test.

When employers use an online test as part of a training programme their intention is typically to explore the results during the subsequent course to aid the individual's development and self-awareness. Online testing in this context feels less threatening since the stakes are lower.

INSIDER INFO

ONLINE RECRUITMENT – THE FUTURE OF JOB APPLICATIONS?

Over the last 10 years online recruitment has replaced high-street recruitment, where you visit a job agency or look in the local paper, as the dominant approach for advertising and accepting applications for jobs.

Websites like Monster and Totaljobs have become the first stop for many employers and candidates in the recruitment market. The busiest time for a jobs site tends to be Monday afternoon around 2pm. This is when the peak numbers of job searches happen – perhaps when people feel most depressed about their current job following the weekend.

Online tests have grown alongside the job sites and employer careers sites. Often you will be passed seamlessly from a website where you completed an online application form or uploaded your CV to an online test site. Once you have completed the test the employer will compare your scores to the information you submitted with your application to make a decision about whether to invite you to interview.

The benefits for employers and candidates tend to be in terms of streamlining and efficiency. It takes less time for employers to process online applications and test results than traditional paper-based approaches. Candidates can be kept up-to-date with the progress of their applications by email and text message.

There is still debate among some business psychologists about whether tests should be used online – but ultimately it is the pragmatism of employers and many candidates that is driving online recruitment and testing. The time savings and conveniences offered by the new technology is causing traditional recruitment and testing to slowly recede.

WHAT IS THE BEST APPROACH TO ACHIEVING YOUR ONLINE PERSONAL BEST?

Here's some advice you should follow if you are asked to complete an online verbal test remotely.

Your testing environment

You can choose where you complete the test from any location that has a web-connected computer. However, to perform at your best you should:

▸ **Choose a quiet, relaxed environment** free from distractions – consider putting a 'do not disturb' sign on your door. Switch off your phone.

▸ **Complete the test in a single sitting**, without taking a break halfway through a test as this will break your concentration. Some online verbal tests will not let you back in to complete a test if you left the system prematurely.

▸ **Give yourself sufficient time** so that you don't have to rush. Most online tests have a strict time-limit – make sure you make the most of the time allowed.

▸ **Focus all of your attention on completing the test**, and ignore any distractions such as the doorbell or phone. If it's important the caller will try again later.

You should aim to make your personal testing session as close in conditions to a traditional, supervised session as possible. This will enable you to perform at your maximum level.

Test-taking strategies

The test-taking strategies you have developed using this book can all be transferred to a remote online verbal test. There are a few additional points, however, that are specific to online tests.

INSIDER INFO

DO PAPER AND PENCIL TEST RESULTS AGREE WITH ONLINE RESULTS?

The short answer is 'broadly yes'. When we correlate test scores gathered using traditional paper and pencil testing under supervised conditions with online verbal test scores gathered using remote testing we see a strong degree of agreement between the two sets of scores. In other words, the results we see from online tests tend to correlate well with traditional test scores.

There is a bit more going on within these findings, however. When we examine individual test scores from the two different types of test administration we see that while most people score the same on both tests, the scores of some candidates do change. Some people's verbal ability scores **decrease** when we test them under supervised conditions and compare this to their initial online performance. But some people's scores actually **increase** when they are tested under supervised conditions compared with their online results.

The important thing to note is that this happens whenever we test a group of people more than once, regardless of the type of test (online or paper and pencil) or type of test administration format (supervised, unsupervised or remote) and compare their results. The results we see tend to be the same for most people but a number of candidates will see an increase or decrease in their second set of test scores.

This is due to practice effects. On the second test session people vary in their approach because of practice – some are more relaxed, some more complacent, some are less anxious and some have developed better test strategies. These factors lie behind the changes we see in some people's test scores.

The good news for you is that this book is built to help you capitalise on these practice effects by developing your test-taking powers to increase your next test score. You can also relax about online tests – they tend to give the same verbal ability results as their traditional, paper and pencil, supervised alternatives.

▶ **Read all on-screen instructions very carefully.** In a traditional supervised test session the administrator will read through the test instructions with you while you read along to ensure you understand how to proceed. With remote testing there is no administrator so it is up to you to ensure you are clear about what you have to do before you start the test itself. There is no time-limit for reading the instructions, so take your time.

▶ **There can be no going back!** Online tests often vary from paper and pencil in their format. Do not make the assumption that the instructions for completing the test are going to be the same as those for a paper and pencil one. One critical example is the use of the 'back' button in your web browser – many online tests prevent you from going back to pages you have already completed to change your answers. This is different from a paper and pencil test where reviewing all your answers once you've attempted all the questions is excellent test-taking strategy. With an online verbal test you should take some time to review your answers before you move on to the next page – you may not be able to go back when you reach the end of the test.

▶ **Untimed tests.** Some online verbal ability tests do not have time-limits. These tests are open-ended and allow you to work at your own pace. In the absence of a time-limit the test will often use other techniques to get a good measurement of your ability, such as questions that become increasingly difficult as you progress through the test. If you complete an untimed test you should still follow the usual test-taking strategy of working quickly but accurately because the length of time you take to complete the test is very likely to be recorded. The time you take to finish may be a factor that is considered alongside your actual verbal ability score. Do not go off to make a cup of tea halfway through a test without a time limit – the clock will still be ticking in the background!

INSIDER INFO

WHY IS STANDARDISATION IMPORTANT?

A traditional testing session takes place under very standardised conditions. This means that the test administrator has to follow the administration instructions for the test very carefully to ensure that the test session is identical in format, approach and timings to every other test session that is conducted using the same verbal test.

One of the reasons for this very standardised approach is to ensure that every candidate receives an equivalent experience to every other candidate, thereby making the assessment fairer.

But there are important psychometric reasons for standardising the testing conditions as well. Test developers need to ensure that test sessions are as close to being identical to each other as possible to maximise the effectiveness and accuracy of the test and the scoring mechanism. In doing so, test developers reduce the numbers of errors within the testing process that might affect your score (upwards or downwards).

When you are taking a test online it is much harder for the test developers to guarantee the same standardisation of testing conditions because they do not take place under supervision. This places demands on the design of the test itself to ensure that it will still measure verbal ability accurately and consistently.

It will benefit your test score if you strive to standardise the conditions of your own online test. This means following the advice above and the instructions for the test very closely.

▶ **Online anxieties.** Most people find remote testing less worrying than supervised testing because of the more relaxed environment and absence of a test administrator. Some people do find it causes them anxiety, however. The test-taking strategies for reducing nerves during a traditional test session still transfer to online testing. Do not worry about a pass/fail score if the verbal test is being used as part of a sifting process prior to the interview – the sifting decision will not be based on your test score alone. Any additional information you have provided, such as your CV, also informs the decision.

Technical advice

You do not need a super-computer to take an online verbal test and a well-designed web-based testing system will not discriminate against you if your computer is getting on a bit. However, there are some points relating to the technology you use that will help you to achieve your personal best.

▶ **Use an up-to-date web browser.** Good online testing systems are designed to run on any computer. The important factor is not the type of computer or its age, but the type of browser you are using. Most people use Microsoft's Internet Explorer because this comes pre-installed on all PCs. Online verbal tests are typically designed to run best on versions of this browser that are newer than version 6. You can check the version of your browser by clicking on 'Help' in its menu bar and selecting 'About Internet Explorer'. Updating to a more recent version is free. If you are using an Apple computer or a different browser on your PC (such as

Firefox or Google's Chrome) then the same advice applies – update to the most recent version. Using older versions of browsers will not stop an online verbal ability test from working but they can cause odd display issues and affect the layout of the test as it appears on your screen – which could potentially affect your score.

▶ **Web-browser settings.** You may experience odd issues if you have custom or unusual settings switched on within your browser. Before taking an online test go to the Options menu and make sure that your browser settings are switched to default. Other settings may cause problems and affect your score.

▶ **Web-connection speed.** You do not need a super-fast connection to take an online test, but a broadband connection will be preferable to a dial-up connection. A slower connection will not affect your score but the frustration of waiting for pages to display might do. Try to use a computer that has a broadband connection.

▶ **No access to a computer.** Not everyone has a computer at home or one they can use at work (especially when applying for alternative employment). The best advice is to use a local library (where internet access is generally free), a friend, family member or colleague's computer, or even an internet café. If you really can't get access to a computer it is the responsibility of the employer who has asked you to complete the test to provide alternative arrangements. Sometimes this involves a paper and pencil version or an appointment to visit the employer and complete the online test at their office.

▶ **No web or computer experience.** Not everyone uses a computer or browses the web. If you do not feel confident taking a test online then the best advice is to contact the employer and ask for an alternative test, such as a paper and pencil one. While it is the test-user's responsibility to ensure all candidates have access to the testing, you should bear in mind that employers will only choose to use an online test if the job itself requires people to use a computer. If you lack confidence or experience with using computers or the internet you may be disadvantaged in terms of your suitability for a job that requires you to use a computer. You could consider developing your computer literacy (see Chapter 9 for suggestions) or alternative jobs that do not require any IT skills.

▶ **Technical difficulties.** Broadband connections tend to be very robust, but if you are using dial-up there is a possibility that you might lose your connection when you are midway through an assessment. If you experience any technical difficulties when completing the online verbal test, such as a dropped web connection or the computer freezing, don't panic! The best advice is to switch your computer off and then switch it back on again. If you leave midway through a timed verbal test you may need to request a reset of the time limit from the individual responsible for the assessment process. You will be guided through this process when you try to resume the assessment. When you re-enter the test system it will either let you pick-up where you left off or invite you to contact a helpdesk. Don't panic – your score will be unaffected. If you are really worried you can ask the employer for another opportunity to take the test, perhaps at their premises.

Cheats never prosper

The temptation to cheat at a remote online verbal test is understandable – a lot can ride on the results and there's no test administrator to keep an eye on what you're up to. The potential for candidate cheating is a source of anxiety for employers who use online tests for remote and high-stakes assessment. Below is a list of the most common forms of cheating at an online verbal test.

> ▸ **Asking a friend to take the test for you.** You might know someone who you feel has higher levels of verbal ability than you, who you could ask to take the test for you. Alternatively you could ask the friend to sit with you while you complete the test or just phone your friend if you encounter any difficult questions. If you use this approach make sure that your friend's verbal ability really is better than your own.
>
> ▸ **Finding the correct answers for the test.** If you know the precise name of the verbal test you will take you could try a web-search for the correct answers. Websites do exist that enable people to share what they believe are the correct answers to widely used online tests – these are sometimes called 'cheat-sheets'. You simply enter these correct multiple-choice answers when you complete the verbal test yourself.
>
> ▸ **Taking the verbal test more than once.** You can complete all the questions in the test as a practice go and then re-apply to the testing system to have another go.

Should you decide to employ any of these methods to improve your test score you should be warned that we test developers

have become very adept at preventing and detecting efforts
to cheat – you will be found out! If you decide to cheat, here's
what you're up against.

> ▶ **Randomised questions.** Most online tests include
>   a degree of randomisation that means the verbal
>   information and questions you are presented with are
>   drawn from a large pool. This means that if you take
>   a verbal test more than once it is unlikely that you
>   will see the same questions. If you try and find the
>   correct answers for an online test the cheat sheet you
>   download is unlikely to match the randomised set of
>   questions and answers you are presented with.
> ▶ **Secure scoring.** Where cheat-sheets do exist they are
>   based on other people's beliefs about what the correct
>   answers to a test actually are. The correct answers to a
>   test are never made public, so cheat sheets may not in
>   fact be an accurate description of the right answers for
>   a test. Widely used verbal tests are frequently updated
>   to stay one step ahead. The questions are changed to
>   minimise any over-familiarity among candidates.
> ▶ **Validation of identity.** Nearly all online tests require a
>   passcode for entry, which is typically only good for one
>   go. This means that if you complete the verbal test once
>   as a practice, you will not be able to get back into the
>   test system to take it again. Online tests take further
>   measures to validate your identity – to ensure it is you
>   who is taking the test and not a friend on your behalf.
> ▶ **Scores can go down as well as up.** If you do manage
>   to fool an online verbal testing system to let you have
>   more than one attempt you should be aware that
>   not everyone's score increases on subsequent goes.

Research into the effects of multiple completion of the same test indicates that for many candidates scores can go down or simply stay the same.

▶ **Verification of results.** If your verbal ability is tested remotely online, any employer who is following simple best practice guidelines will retest your verbal ability under supervision to verify the results. This retesting can take the form of a paper and pencil test, a supervised online test when you attend interview or a different assessment method entirely. It is not unusual for employers to use a written exercise or role-play exercise alongside the interview to verify your level of verbal ability. If your online test score was inflated through cheating you will be found out!

If you try to cheat at an online test all or one of these measures will find you out!

We test developers have a number of other measures that are designed to deter, resist and detect efforts to cheat so on balance our advice would be don't try your luck. If you are fortunate enough to cheat at a verbal test and get the job, remember that your new employer will expect to see you demonstrate the same level of verbal ability in your performance at work as your online test score.

All methods of testing, selection and assessment are open to abuse by candidates who want to get the job, not least the interview. Ultimately it is in your best interests to be honest and avoid ending up in a role to which you are not suited in terms of your verbal ability.

CHAPTER 7

WHAT HAPPENS AFTER TAKING THE TEST?

W hat a weight off your mind – you've completed the verbal test and now you can relax! But just because the test is over doesn't mean that you can forget about it. There are opportunities to develop your personal best verbal test score further still if you make the right use of any results that are communicated to you.

In order to develop your personal best score based on your verbal test results you need to understand a little more about test scores, what they mean and how to maximise the benefit you gain from any feedback about your performance.

HOW TEST RESULTS ARE USED

Test scores should never be used in isolation. Whether the verbal test was used as part of a recruitment or development process, the results should always be placed in the context of other information about you.

This might mean combining your verbal test results with scores from another test, such as a numerical test, or with a different type of assessment entirely such as a personality questionnaire or interview.

When placed into context with other assessments of your ability and/or personality your verbal test score can tell you something about how your ability in this area integrates with your other strengths or weaknesses. This overall interpretation enables potential employers to make a more informed selection decision about you, or if the test formed part of a development process it will enable you to develop greater self-awareness.

The test user should offer you feedback about your verbal test results but this will often be in the context of a wider set of results. Within this feedback you need to understand what the results mean if you are to interpret and learn from your verbal test score.

WHAT THE RESULTS MEAN

Your verbal test score is unlikely to be simply the number of questions you answered correctly. Your results will be calculated on the basis of how your performance compares with people who have taken the same verbal test before.

This comparison group will be made up of people whose background, educational level or job is broadly representative of candidates who are taking the test for the employer who has asked you to complete the assessment. Typically the group will comprise over 100 people whose performance on the test will range from excellent to poor.

This comparison enables the test-user to understand how strong your verbal ability is in relation to other people. The comparison consists of a calculation that produces your verbal ability result.

Typically this result is framed in terms of how well you performed compared to other people. It is unlikely that you will be given a numerical score or grade as you would with an educational test. Instead the test-user will describe your result in terms of how close it is to the average score. Here are some examples of how real verbal test scores are fed back to candidates.

'Your verbal ability is well above average compared to a group of managers who have taken the test before.'

'Your verbal test result lies within the bottom 20% of other graduates who applied to the same role.'

'Your verbal ability lies within the average range for call centre workers; it is typical of other people working in call centre roles.'

The test-user will not feedback the number of questions you answered correctly because this is not the way that the results from modern psychometric tests of verbal ability are scored and interpreted. In the case of online tests, where the scoring is conducted automatically by the computer, the test-user is unlikely to know how many questions you answered right or wrong. Your results will be presented in terms of the comparison to other test takers.

GETTING THE MOST FROM TEST FEEDBACK

Only trained test-users should feedback your results. This ensures that the feedback you receive is based on expert knowledge of the test and what its results mean. While the verbal test score itself is generally the piece of information with which candidates are most preoccupied, the broader feedback process has much greater potential for helping you improve on your verbal test performance in future.

Verbal test feedback is an excellent opportunity to discover the detail identified about your verbal ability by the test. Based on my experience and the experiences of other occupational

INSIDER INFO

PERCENTILE SCORING

The majority of verbal test results are based on a scoring system called percentiles. A percentile score tells you what proportion of people who've taken the test before you have scored better than (or worse than!).

The comparison group of people who have taken the test before is called a 'norm group'. Your performance on the verbal test is compared with the norm group and the resulting percentile score describes your verbal ability in relation to this group.

So, if you score on the 75th percentile you scored better than three-quarters of the norm group – or you are in the top 25%. If you scored on the 50th percentile you are better than the bottom half of the norm group, but worse then the top half (the 50th percentile is the absolute average in percentile terms but most test-users interpret any percentile score between the 35th and 64th as lying in the average range of ability).

It is important not to confuse percentile scores with percentage scores. A percentile score tells you how well you performed in relation to others; it does not tell you what percentage of the test questions you scored correctly.

The composition of the norm group your performance is being compared with is an important piece of information in terms of understanding your verbal ability percentile score. You should be compared with a group of people who are similar to you in terms of educational level, work experience and the type of job for which you've applied. Ideally the norm group will be made up of people who have taken the test for the same employer as you have and for the same purpose or job.

A trained test-user will be able to clearly explain your percentile score and the nature of the norm group with which you've been compared during the feedback process.

psychologists and expert test-users, here are some points to bear in mind when receiving test feedback.

▶ **Be honest.** The test-user providing your feedback may prompt you to describe your reactions to the test and how you feel your results will look. It will help improve the quality of the feedback discussion if you are honest with yourself and the feedback provider about your experiences of the test and your prediction of your performance. Sharing your experience of the test will enable the test-user to shape the feedback to help you identify the aspects of your performance that could be improved next time. If, for example, you found the verbal test difficult or confusing then tell the test user. This is useful information that they can use to help you develop your approach in future.

▶ **Don't be defensive.** The test user will feedback your results using the kind of language described above – how your performance compares to other candidates. This means that the test-user may use terms like 'below average', or 'bottom 15%' to describe your results. Receiving feedback can be an emotional process and you should put any defensive reactions to one side. Avoid arguing about the outcome – remember that psychometric verbal ability tests have very high levels of reliability, and their measurements tend to be very accurate. If your test result is a surprise (perhaps lower than you expected) then you should use the feedback discussion to identify the reasons that may have contributed to the result. This might give you a clue about how to improve your performance next time.

▶ **Ask follow-up questions.** You can ask the feedback provider to describe what your verbal ability test score means in relation to the job. If the test was used for recruitment purposes the test-user should be able to describe what elements of the role would be affected by your test results. Where the verbal test is being used as part of a development process you should ask the test-user to identify the implications that the result has for your future development – do the results suggest a development need for your verbal ability?

▶ **Ask for advice.** The feedback provider should be able to provide you with advice for improving your future test performance that is specific to the test you have taken. You can prompt the test-user to identify actions you could take to improve your test-taking strategy, your knowledge of the specific verbal test used and your underlying verbal ability.

Test-users are encouraged by test developers and the British Psychological Society to always offer feedback to test takers. Not every employer adopts this best-practice approach though it is always worth confirming before taking the test whether test feedback will be available. Chapter 8 explores rights such as these that you should expect to be fulfilled as a test-taker.

INSIDER INFO

BEST PRACTICE IN ABILITY TEST FEEDBACK

During the feedback test-users who have qualified with the British Psychological Society to use ability tests are trained to:

▶ Reiterate **why the test was used**.

▶ Describe the **role of the test score** in any selection decision.

▶ Provide a short but clear **description of the test**.

▶ Explain issues of **confidentiality and data storage** regarding your test results.

▶ Ensure that feedback is an **interactive** process in which the test-user discusses the findings with the test-user.

▶ Describe the results in **clear, lay terms**.

▶ **Relate the result to the position** for which you've applied.

▶ Ask for your **comments and reactions**.

▶ Provide you with an opportunity to **ask questions** about your test results.

As a test-taker you should expect the feedback you receive to reflect this best-practice approach.

CHAPTER 8
YOUR TESTING RIGHTS

P sychometric tests of ability should only be used by trained specialists. This might be an occupational psychologist or someone who holds recognised occupational testing qualifications. Trained test-users should stick to testing best-practice principles that ensure your testing rights are met.

As with any technology, tests can be abused by people who have not been properly trained or who simply do not conform to best practice. As a test-taker you should be aware of your testing rights and testing best practice more generally. When a test is misused or best practice ignored, the measurement of your ability is likely to be distorted or misinterpreted. It is very difficult to achieve your personal best score under such circumstances.

HOW YOU SHOULD BE TREATED

A key principle in testing is 'informed consent'. As a test-taker you have a right to be fully informed about the nature of the assessment process before you give your consent to be tested. This means that the test-user must provide you with these key pieces of information before you consent to take the test.

> ▶ **What the test measures.** In this case they would tell you that it is a test of your verbal ability.
> ▶ **What the results will be used for.** The test-user must be clear about how the test results will be used within their recruitment or development process. The results must never be used for purposes other than those to which you have consented.
> ▶ **Who will see your results.** The test-user must provide clear assurances about the boundaries of

confidentiality around your test results. This means being clear about who will see you test scores.

▶ **How long your results will be stored.** You need to be told how long the employer will hold on to your results – 6–12 months is a typical length of time.

▶ **Provision of feedback.** The employer must be clear about whether or not they will provide feedback. Best practice is to offer feedback to all candidates, but many employers feel unable to do so because of high volumes or lack of resources. Many employers therefore provide feedback on request to unsuccessful candidates and encourage feedback to be taken up by successful ones. Other employers offer no feedback at all. Your fundamental right as a test-taker is to have a clear understanding about what feedback, if any, will be available once you have completed your verbal test.

Usually this information should be provided when the employer contacts you to invite you to complete the test. The letter will either ask you to confirm that you consent to be tested or require you to contact the employer if there are any conditions you are not happy with.

Hand-in-hand with this right to informed consent you have certain responsibilities as a test-taker. If there are any factors which might affect your test performance you must let the test-user know so that they can make any appropriate adjustments. Common candidate needs of this kind are impaired vision, dyslexia or language difficulties. If you feel that your test performance may be adversely affected by factors such as these, it is your responsibility to bring them to the attention of the test-user before the testing session. Only this way can the test-user take actions that will ensure you are able to demonstrate your personal best.

As a test-taker you should also expect to not be adversely affected by the experience of being tested. This is called the 'principle of self-regard', which states that test-takers should feel as good about themselves at the end of a test session as they did at the beginning. Test-takers have a responsibility to ensure that testing is appropriate, related to the job and not excessive.

If you experience a test session that you feel breaks the principle of self-regard you might consider whether the employer is an attractive one to be working for.

TESTING BEST PRACTICE

The BPS has established a set of standards that test users should adhere to in order to ensure that tests are used in a fair, effective and ethical way. Test-users must hold the BPS qualification in occupational testing called Level A in order to use ability tests.

When you are invited to a testing session you can check whether the employer holds this Level A training by contacting the BPS, who keep a register of qualified test users (details are given in Chapter 9). Individuals who are not Level A qualified are unlikely to adhere to the levels of best practice that you should expect as a test-taker. The testing may not be fair, effective or ethical.

Level A trained test-users will also understand the nature and quality of different verbal tests and select the one that is most relevant and appropriate for their testing purposes. Trained test-users know which tests to avoid on the basis of quality or reliability.

The BPS standards were established to protect test-takers from being subjected to unfair, inappropriate and unethical test use. You can find out more about the standards from the BPS website.

CHAPTER 9
FURTHER RESOURCES

T here is more help and support out there for test-takers. Once you have worked through this book you may find it helpful to continue your preparation using the resources below.

PRACTICE RESOURCES

Practice questions provided by test publishers can be found at:

▶ http://criterionpartnership.co.uk/psychometrics_help
▶ www.shldirect.com/practice_tests.html

TEST SOPHISTICATION RESOURCES

Advice on how to approach tests can be found at:

▶ http://criterionpartnership.co.uk/takers_advice
▶ www.shlgroup.com
▶ www.savilleconsulting.com/products/aptitude_ preparationguides.aspx
▶ www.psychtesting.org.uk/ptc/roles$/the-public.cfm

TEST KNOWLEDGE RESOURCES

For further information about testing and good practice try:

▶ The British Psychological Society (BPS) Psychological Testing Centre. This is the body that promotes test standards. A number of useful resources can be found on their website, including the 'Level A standards –

test-takers guide' and the BPS register of qualified test
users: www.psychtesting.org.uk/

▶ The International Test Commission (ITC). The ITC
has established a set of standards for online testing,
'International guidelines on computer-based and
Internet delivered tests', which you can find at: www.
intestcom.org/guidelines/index.php